KU-223-551

NEVERTHELESS

'Debt is so often a relationship breaker. It destroys families and leaves individuals feeling there is no hope. I cannot tell you how strongly I feel about the work that CAP does. As I walked around CAP's HQ, there were tears in my eyes as I saw the reality of thousands of lives changed forever. In 'Nevertheless' we have a thrilling account of how God got hold of one man, John Kirkby, and through him reached out to the most needy in our society. This book is a roller-coaster ride filled with passion, faith and hope.'

Rob Parsons
Care for the Family

'John's life and the story of CAP can be summed up in two words: "Why not?". When it comes to the eradication of poverty, "Why not now?", "Why not us?", "Why not CAP?". I have worked with thousands of organisations, but CAP is one of the best examples I've seen of a Christian charity that is effectively combining professionalism with a real heart for God, and reaching the lost with the love and grace of Christ. You will be inspired by this story!'

Malcolm Duncan
Leader of Faithworks

'When I first heard CAP's story a few years ago, something resounded in my heart. This story is an amazing example of what God can achieve when a person moves the ideas from their heart and mind to their hands and feet. I am so encouraged to see CAP here in Australia and beginning to spread throughout the world. This story must be told to remind us just what God can achieve in this modern twenty-first Century society.'

Mark Zschech

'John's story is one of victory over adversity when the spirit of God was released into a broken man's life. Christians Against Poverty is now one of the most significant ministries I have come across for some time. You will be amazed, challenged and inspired to see how CAP has grown to become a world changing ministry that has always taken its lead from God.

Debt is amongst the most pressing issues affecting western societies in the twenty-first Century, and one that the church has been slow to respond to. You will read how, through CAP, churches across the world have had the unique opportunity to respond with a practical demonstration of God's love, liberating people from the oppression and shame of debt. This book stands as a testimony to how God can use individuals to turn the tide.

I count it a privilege to support John as CAP continues to grow in Australia, New Zealand and around the world. Through partnering with CAP, our church continues to reach out to our community in a dynamic way. My prayer is that you will be inspired to do the same as you read 'Nevertheless'.

Pastor Phil Pringle
Christian City Church
Oxford Falls, Australia

'If you like a good human story, you'll love this! It is the story of one life, but, more importantly in many ways, the potential that one life had to influence so many more. What makes it remarkable is the relatively short period it covers. John was saved in 1992 and CAP was only founded in 1996! If God can do so much through one life dedicated to his purpose in those few years, what can he do through a lifetime? John's story will inspire you to get in touch with that which God wants you to do for him in your lifetime and get on with it. Who knows what you will encounter along the way? Only God, and as you tenaciously hold onto his promise, one day you too will say, "Nevertheless God's word is sure!"'

Stephen Matthew
Associate Pastor
Abundant Life Church, Bradford

NEVERTHELESS

*The incredible story of
one man's mission to change
thousands of people's lives*

JOHN KIRKBY

CHRISTIANS AGAINST POVERTY BOOKS
Bradford

Copyright © John Kirkby 2003, 2006, 2008, 2009, 2010

First published 2003
Reprinted 2005
Second edition 2006
Reprinted 2007
Third Edition 2008
Reprinted 2009
Fourth Edition 2009
Fifth Edition 2010

Published by Christians Against Poverty Books,
Jubilee Mill, North Street, Bradford, BD1 4EW

ISBN 978-0-9546410-3-0

All rights reserved.
No part of this publication may be reproduced or
transmitted in any form or by any means, electronic
or mechanical, including photocopy, recording or any
information storage or retrieval system, without
permission in writing from the publisher.

Biblical quotations are taken from
NIV – New International Version © 1973,
1978, 1984 by the International Bible Society; and from
RSV – Revised Standard Version copyrighted 1946, 1952, © 1971,
1973 by the Division of Christian Education and Ministry of the
National Council of the Churches of Christ In the USA.
LITV - Literal Translation of the Holy Bible, copyright © 1976 - 2000,
by Jay P. Green, Sr, used by permission of the copyright holder.

Book design by Christians Against Poverty.

CONTENTS

INTRODUCTION

Welcome to the amazing story of how God transformed my life, how Christians Against Poverty was born and how it has grown. As it unfolds you will read of my early life, how I became a Christian, and a history of the events, people and struggles encountered as we founded and established the charity.

I am grateful for the individuals who have given me permission to include their names and those who have been brave enough to let me use their testimonies. Obviously, this is how I have seen things. It's my personal perception of events, and others may have seen them differently. Some of the diary accounts were written in the midst of some difficult and amazing times and are a little raw in places. My intention is simply to give you a true feel for what was going on.

I want to say a very special thank you to Tina Morris, Jonathan Priestley and Claire Cowles who work in our Communications Team, and who have worked with me to update each edition turning it into the version you read today. I also want to thank Marianne Clough who helped me complete the first edition. She is a great supporter and encourager of both CAP and myself. It was her insistence that 'we only have one chance to tell this story right' that inspired me to complete the first book.

This book is dedicated to my wonderful, supportive and loving wife Lizzie, who has stuck with me through thick and thin; to my five children Jasmine, Jessica, Abigail, Thomas and Lydia Joy. Also to my faithful mum who passed away in 2005 after a year-long battle with cancer. She is sadly missed and remembered fondly by all who had the privilege of knowing her. To the man who brought me to the Lord, and had such a tremendous influence on my life, Paul Hubbard. It is also dedicated to my great friends and co-workers Matt and Josie Barlow, who have been by my side through every challenge since 1999, and to all CAP staff and supporters past and present. Without their combined belief in and support of the vision God placed in me, this story could not have been told.

Finally, and most importantly, I dedicate this book to my Lord and Saviour Jesus Christ. Without his wonderful faithful presence, guidance, wisdom and encouragement there would simply be nothing to write about.

My prayer is that your faith in the Lord is increased and that your understanding of how he can work is broadened. I pray also that you will sense the awesome deeds he can perform through normal men and women just like you and me.

To him be all the glory, honour and praise.

CHAPTER ONE

JOHN KIRKBY: THE EARLY YEARS

The Early Years

I was born in the West Yorkshire town of Heckmondwike on October 25, 1961. As a family we were members of the United Reformed Church there. My mum, who had a great faith, took me along every Sunday, but although I knew about God I had no real understanding of who he really was.

My sisters Susan and Judith were twelve and thirteen years older than me. Both had flown the nest by the time I was seven and I enjoyed the attention of both my parents as if I had been an only child.

My dad was from a fairly poor background but had worked his way up through a seven-year apprenticeship to be an electrician, and then over fifteen years to become an electrical engineer for the BBA Group in nearby Cleckheaton. The firm made brake linings and conveyor belts. He was an eccentric and handsome man with half-rimmed glasses who was forever tinkering with electronics. He actually invented several things that had successful patents, one being a gadget to prevent people cutting their hands on a machinery blade. If you had ventured into the loft of our otherwise ordinary three-bed semi, you would have found it filled with the most impressive model railway that my dad had built and completely automated. He would come down for tea leaving six tracks worth of trains eerily stopping and starting by themselves without ever bumping into each other.

I was the son he had always wanted and because I arrived later on in his life he had a lot of time to spend with me. He was willing to go fishing, exploring, and I have lovely memories of us damming rivers and that kind of thing. As a young child I was his constant companion and his loving and gentle nature was a great influence on me during my early life.

My mum cared enormously for me and tried hard to keep me on the straight and narrow, though not always very successfully. She was always kind and generous and very forgiving, which was a good thing.

John with his father, Donald, proudly showing their catch of fish

During the last nine years of his life, my father had long spells in hospital and my mum looked after me. Great parents are so valuable and I have so much to thank mine for. They brought me up in a loving environment, helped me to develop healthy self-eteem and encouraged me in everything I did. I was really blessed and it left me very secure.

I was bright at school despite mild dyslexia. On the streets I was confident and popular. I lost my front tooth and picked up several scars in the process of holding my own – the fighting spirit was quite literally alive in me from the start.

I left church aged eleven as soon as my mum finally said I could. However, I had a definite re-awakening of my faith when I was fourteen during a showing of the film 'The Cross and the Switchblade' at a local church. It told the true story of how a young pastor took on a dead inner-city church surrounded by gangs and drugs and changed many lives through it.

After the film, I remember standing in front of my mates with tears running down my face. I went forward and spent some time with a young lad who explained it was Jesus, and I think I prayed the prayer of salvation. My mum's church minister tried his best to get hold of me, and I went to at least one bible group and a young peoples' group twice. After that, the pull of the world and my mates just drew me back.

Only God knows what would have happened to me if I had continued with the faith he had obviously stirred in me. I feel this particularly as I see my eldest daughter Jasmine, with a real faith and a world of opportunity before her. Even though I gave up on God, he never gave up on me.

When I was just nine, my father – a teetotaller – contracted a virus that led to a serious liver illness, which brought about his death nine years later when he was just fifty-seven. My father was very ill for the majority of my teenage years, and I have to say I was by no means a perfect son. I was quite rebellious with a gift for getting into trouble and I steadily progressed through all the vices such as drugs and alcohol. He was in hospital for long periods of time and I would visit whenever I could. I now know that the true extent of his illness was kept from me until near his death. One of my greatest regrets is that in the years running up to his death he may have seen me as a rebellious, ungrateful, selfish teenager. I often wonder what he thought of his beloved son when he saw me making such a mess of my life. I hope he saw through all that and believed I would come good one day.

I still miss him and can easily be overcome emotionally with the loss. It's one of those things that doesn't get easier for me with the passing of time. Since the birth of my fourth child Tommy (full name Thomas Donald after his Granddad) in 2001, my sense of loss has been increased. My dad was forty when I was born, the same age I was when Tommy turned up. When I play with and spend such fun times with Tommy, I often think of the love my dad must have had for me. How he must have loved me as I love my son. It is a hard thing to lose your father so early on.

Aged 1¹/₂: 1963 elections. Dad stood as prospective Liberal councillor

My working life begins

Heckmondwike Grammar School's headmaster was in shock at the six O-Levels I achieved there. Certainly I hadn't shown a great deal of promise in the run-up to them. But the fighting spirit came through again for me and I had crammed all the way to the finish after appalling mock exam results. Not bad for someone who had almost 'opted out' of school a year earlier.

At fifteen I took extra time off school over the summer to work at a local paint factory where I told them I was sixteen. I made up a National Insurance number by jumbling up my mate's letters and numbers, so someone somewhere owes me some contributions! They took me on to be a 'lidder' (yes, that's where you bang a lid on a paint tin with a wooden mallet!). After a couple of weeks I got promoted to a 'stacker' (where you stack full tins of paint on a pallet!). A few weeks later I reached the highest level within the team, a 'filler' (I had to open and close a pipe with a lever to fill tins of paint). It may not have been the most impressive career start but at least I got the top job. However, the job was the easy bit.

Care for employees and Health and Safety had not reached Norman Driver Surface Coatings in the 1970s. Violence and bullying were endemic and I literally had to fight other lads to avoid being beaten and bullied. Had my mum and dad known what I faced I know they would have got me out.

I hardened up very quickly and although I would never wish this type of experience on any young person, it did make me realise that life was going to be a bit tougher than I had thought. If I was to get on, I would need to use all my wits, work hard and wise up very quickly.

One job no one else in the factory wanted to do was to take the sandwich orders, but I remember jumping at the chance to get out for an hour or two. Within days I had negotiated with two sandwich firms, got them to knock their prices down and was pocketing the difference – entrepreneurial or what! After eight weeks of this I returned to school to see out the last few months, a little humbled by what the real world was like.

After my O-Levels, I took a commercial apprenticeship with a local engineering company and for the next two years learned basic office systems and studied, somewhat unsuccessfully, for an ONC in Business Studies at Huddersfield College.

My father died quite suddenly on February 3, 1980. He had seemed to recover many times before only to lapse back into serious illness. This had become normal to us all. He was a real fighter who never complained but just fought and fought and I got used to the fact that he kept getting better. But one day he didn't and died peacefully in his sleep. I was the first to reach the hospital, and as I looked into his face and held his hand somehow he looked at rest. I think that after such a hard nine-year battle his body just said, 'I have had enough.'

It was a traumatic time for the whole family. My mum managed to be very strong for us all but within a year it became too much for her to bear. She had a nervous breakdown and had to go into hospital for many weeks. This left me aged nineteen, living at home on my own and visiting her in hospital while trying to progress in a new and very demanding job.

I crammed all the great care-free time you have in your late teens into the weekends. I had a motorbike and leathers and was into heavy music, 'drugs and rock and roll', and all that goes with it. I was basically off the rails from Friday to Sunday.

I met my first wife, Anne, in a rock club in Dewsbury about two months after my dad's death. We married in 1982 after three years together. We were just twenty and twenty-one. When we first got together she was doing teacher training in Scarborough. She was beautiful, relaxed and great fun. I would finish work on a Friday and race up to Scarborough with my mates to spend wild weekends sleeping in the back of vans, roughing it and wondering at the student culture I was missing out on. Then I would be haring back home in the early hours of Monday morning with enough time to change into my suit and tie ready for the sensible day job.

Around the time of my dad's death, I had what turned out to be a decisive career change. I just got sick of boring office work and walked into the Brighouse Job Centre one dinnertime. I saw a job for an "Accounts Representative" with an American finance company called Avco Trust. I applied and got the job. It turned out that it was a posh name for a debt collector and loan salesman.

The company was very good at training and I learned a lot of basic skills in managing people, businesses, dealing with the public and how the finance industry worked. They were not interested in academic achievement. They wanted to know if you would work hard and get results. They had competitions and were really success orientated, and I thrived in that environment. Over the next two years I got stuck in and discovered what I was good at – communicating and dealing with people, working very hard, getting things done and making things happen. I had a rapid rise within the company and at twenty-one became the manager of their Doncaster office, one of the youngest they had ever had. Over the next seven years I had a very successful career with Avco, running several branches, and I continued to prosper in both business and at home.

As I reflect on this time, it's obvious to me that I had no real idea of the misery some customers were going through. I was just trying hard to do my job. This has helped me over the years to deal with and understand the finance industry.

During this time, my first daughter Jasmine was born in September 1986. The birth of your first child must rank as one of the most amazing experiences of your life. To hold my own daughter in my hands was something I will never forget. Right from the word go she was so bright, sharp and quick to learn. She walked at seven months and you could have an adult conversation with her when she was just eighteen months old. Jasmine has grown into a wonderful young woman of whom I am very proud.

My second daughter Jessica came along in 1990. She is so full of life, with a very gentle and loving nature. She is very bright and full of grace and compassion for others. Jessica is growing up and making the most of her life; we are great mates and go skiing together. She is such a laugh and fun to be with.

By now I had left Avco and I worked for a year setting up and pioneering a new contract hire and leasing company in the motor trade. Unfortunately my boss treated me appallingly and I was unceremoniously sacked. Determined never to work for anyone ever again, I started my own business – building, hiring and selling sun beds, and working from my garage. This idea came from one of the companies I had helped get vehicles for and I was staggered by the amount of money they were making. My sister Susan and brother-in-law Stewart joined me after a couple of years and we became the largest sun bed retailer in the north of England. I then began to expand into numerous, ultimately less successful, businesses. I grew my own small finance company that financed the sun bed sales, and I also started a financial services company and a loan brokerage company. I even experimented with building and selling houses. Last, but by no means least, I started an estate agency business.

As I look back on that time, I am overwhelmed by how much of an entrepreneurial spirit God had given me and I learned so much about turning ideas into reality. However, without wisdom and left unchecked, it eventually resulted in my businesses collapsing. I had everything the world deems successful; a beautiful wife, two lovely children, a six bedroom secluded house, cars, holidays and money in the bank. But it was all built on sand with nothing underneath it, as I was soon to find out.

In early 1992 my whole world fell apart. I made many mistakes and had borrowed huge sums of money to finance my business operations. Banks started to ask for their money back and a house I had built plummeted in value before I could sell it. I might have looked fine on the outside but inside I was a broken, lonely man watching all I had worked for being lost before my very eyes.

One day my accountant told me that I should go bankrupt as my interest payments and overheads were so huge and my assets had become almost worthless. Every day I had to manage several businesses and juggle huge sums of money just to get through. I used credit cards to pay wages and suppliers. It was a crazy time of ever increasing problems, pressure and difficulties. Something had to give. However, there was one glimmer of hope as we were very close to selling the estate agency for £30,000.

Things had looked very rosy when I started the estate agency with a friend in the late 1980s, but the collapse of the housing market just destroyed us. We had increasing debts of over £30,000 that we had borrowed to keep the business afloat, and the lease on our shop had four years to run. The landlord was threatening to sue us for the whole four years rent of over £25,000. We agreed to sell the business for £30,000 to a company backed by Sun Alliance and this would have cleared our debts. They would also take over the lease we had on the premises. This would have given me half a chance, as the other businesses were relatively sound. The day before we were due to complete I was informed that the deal was off due to increased nervousness in the housing market.

I climbed into my beloved 2.8i Granada Scorpio, I switched off my mobile, started her up and instinctively started to drive home. A few hundred yards from our house I pulled off the road into a pub car park and passed out with physical and emotional stress. Anne was driving six year old Jasmine home from school when she spotted her daddy's car and they pulled over. I remember being woken by Jasmine knocking on my car window saying, 'Daddy, Daddy wake up.' Anne took me home and I collapsed, and went into a semi-coma for two days. I alone knew what this all meant for us as a family, and the pain was excruciating. As I sit and write this book it still makes me shudder to remember how I felt. Virtually everything had been lost and I found myself with huge debts totalling over £78,000 and nowhere to turn.

Over the next week I came round to the fact and I somehow managed to pull myself together. Something inside (perhaps the 'nevertheless' spirit, which I now know God had given me) said, 'I will not go under without a fight.' I began to do what I could to minimise the difficulties. I knew I was fighting a losing battle yet I was determined to carry on. I wasn't to know that, just around the corner, I was about to encounter the living God, my Saviour, in a most dramatic way.

CHAPTER TWO

GOD STEPS IN:
JOHN BECOMES A CHRISTIAN

I had a four-bedroomed detached house in Baildon, North Bradford, which I had ended up with thanks to a brave but foolhardy property deal. It had a huge mortgage on it and I was desperate to sell it to reduce my interest payments and get rid of one more headache.

One Saturday I received a phone call from a bloke who said he was a pastor who had just come over from his wife's home country, Norway. He and his young family had nowhere to live and he wanted to know if he could rent my house. This man, Pastor Paul Hubbard, was to become one of the most influential people in my life. I remember thinking, 'A pastor as a tenant is the last thing I need!'

How wrong could I have been! Over a period of a few months I got to know Paul and his wife Kjersti. They invited me to their home and befriended me. Despite my problems, I became involved in their struggles. They had nothing when they arrived. I even bought them some carpets with some of the rent they paid as they had so little. However they seemed so at peace with life and so open and caring towards my family and me.

Then on the evening of Wednesday 24 June 1992, as I collected my rent, Paul simply gave me a Bible and said they had been praying for

me. He asked, 'Would you like to come to our church on Sunday?' I
took the Bible and said, 'Yes, I will.'

As I walked in the door that night I felt different. Anne was the first
to notice it as soon as I came in. She said, 'What's happened to you?'

I went to church on 5 July 1992. It was a small church in Shipley,
north of Bradford, called Charlestown Baptist. I just knew there was
something there I was supposed to yield to. I now know this was the
love of Jesus reaching out to one needy man. Paul asked me back for
a coffee and I gave my life to the Lord in his kitchen. I was baptised in
December 1992.

Being baptised by Derrick Clarke: 6 December 1992,
Charlestown Baptist Church

Who would have thought that when I put that house up for sale, God
would come knocking on my door! I was instantly on fire for him. I

actually began visiting sick people in Bradford Royal Infirmary with a guy called Martin Jones. We just went onto wards and started talking to and praying for sick people we didn't even know. I also remember being on an outreach and stopping cars at a roundabout to give them tracts and talking to them about Jesus. (Zealot or what!)

We moved with the majority of the congregation in February 1996 to start Christian Life Church in Shipley. It was in this church that CAP was born a few months later.

Back to 1992. At this point, newly saved, I know that I'm supposed to say my life went from strength to strength but the truth is somewhat different. I was about to embark on what were to become among the most difficult two years of my life.

Although saved, I was still living in between the world and the Lord. I was really mixed up and did many things I later regretted. I may well have been the worst new Christian ever! Whenever I hear of new or long-standing Christians having difficulties, I always think back to how far short I fell, and still fall, as a Christian. Perhaps that's how God gives us the grace and compassion we need for our brothers and sisters when they struggle.

My financial situation continued to worsen. It wasn't one aspect of the business that was going into melt-down, it was many all at the same time. The unthinkable was being played out in front of me, regardless of the efforts I made.

This pressure and my past mistakes were to be the seeds of our eventual marriage breakdown, as we simply grew apart.

I used to look out of the window and see my girls playing in the garden knowing in my heart their parents' marriage was over and I'd lost them their home. I felt so guilty and incredibly ashamed that I'd had so much and blown the lot. My accountant said I needed to find £1,000 a week to meet the interest payments or face bankruptcy. The stresses took their toll on my marriage and in February 1994, Anne and I separated. However, to this day we remain good friends and have both worked hard to keep things amicable between us. I praise God for the positive relationship we have managed to maintain for the sake of our beautiful daughters.

Over the next year I gradually fell apart. I was a completely broken man, living in a shell, shattered and breaking up. I used to look after my two girls Jasmine, then aged seven, and Jessica, four, every alternate weekend from Friday to Sunday and one night a week. I lived in a room at my friend Stan's house, where he looked after me and was very supportive. When the girls stayed we had to use two camp beds in my one small room. I would often cry just looking at them both asleep next to me. The word 'destitute' is often over used but that is what I became, utterly devoid of any spirit, hurting, lonely and afraid. I now know that God used this and other desperate experiences in my life for good. It was through these traumatic times that a greater sense of his love, forgiveness and heart for me became more and more real. I also began to have an ever-increasing compassion for others who were in need.

If you have ever been unsympathetic towards a single parent or judged them for struggling, try it yourself for just a couple of days. If you are a single parent my heart goes out to you and I pray you will be strengthened as you try so hard alone. God knows your struggles and he is there to help you.

If right now you are thinking, 'I'm in no fit state to serve God and I will never get into a place where God can use me,' be encouraged. Can you ever imagine anybody less likely to be able to start a Christian ministry and see his past so dramatically used for God's glory as me? I remain to this day a man who can struggle and who has weaknesses and difficulties, but still he uses me. There is no one beyond the love and hope that is in Jesus.

Over the next two years God helped me resurrect my career in the consumer finance industry working for Welcome Financial Services, a company I helped start back in the late 1980s. I was running their secured lending department, which we started in Bradford. It grew very rapidly and was the first place I began to see the blessing of God in my life. If it wasn't for this job and the earning potential I then possessed,

I know that the companies who I owed money to would have pushed me into bankruptcy. I still owed huge debts to various companies and I had to contact all my creditors and make arrangements to pay reduced repayments. Most were helpful. But I needed everything I could muster to stop some of them taking me to court. A court order would have meant me losing my job. They knew it and used it against me. I would never have thought in those dark days that God was preparing me for what was to come. I was actually doing for myself what CAP was about to do for thousands of other people and I had no idea.

I can now see that my work was indeed blessed by God and we became one of the most profitable departments within the company. Due to a very generous profit share and fantastic salary I was able to rapidly reduce my debts, which had reached about £78,000 in 1992, down to £25,000 at the beginning of 1996. Praise the Lord for his provision.

The business of helping people to borrow money was making me feel more and more uneasy. I often dealt with people unable to pay back what they had borrowed and who were really struggling. My Christian heart was telling me to help them and I did what I could for them by reducing or stopping interest and accepting reduced payments. I also had to be responsible to my employers and remain professional.

It was during this time that I started to get myself more and more sorted out with God in terms of getting my life in line with his word. I began to put the teaching I was getting into practice in my life. It took me about two years from being saved to get my head around the whole area of tithing and giving. I eventually understood that God provided me with all my income and let me keep up to ninety per cent.

We often expect new Christians to get themselves sorted out immediately, to get a huge revelation from the moment they receive Christ. If that happens, then praise God, but most people need time to allow God to renew their minds. We then get his revelation through his grace and patience. Why do we often expect everyone else to get a revelation in a few minutes when it has taken us years to get it? Let's get real. It takes most people time and grace to get things firmly established within them, it's a 'life' process.

I am often reminded, very gently and graciously by the Lord, that I have just scratched the surface of his understanding and that there is plenty more for me to learn. No doubt I will get it wrong again in the future.

In March 1995, a strange and wonderful thing happened. Paul and Kjersti Hubbard were in their car parked at Bradford Christian School, when they saw a young woman walking from the pre-school where she worked. They both looked at each other and said, 'There's John's future wife.' They were very sensible and arranged for us to meet with a few friends for a pizza and see what happened. Lizzie had no idea that Paul and Kjersti were orchestrating the event so we could meet. The first thing I noticed about Lizzie was her face, so bright and joyful. She wore a long denim dress with a little flower patch on it, and she was constantly followed by the small group of children who were there. I was captivated and I invited her to my house for a barbecue. She had something very special about her. It shone out of her.

Lizzie brought me alive. I was completely besotted with her and her gentle spirit of love towards me. She accepted me like no one else. She was six years younger than me and single. She had become a committed Christian seven years earlier. She has said, in jest I hope, that she was waiting for 'a knight in shining armour to sweep her off her feet' and got 'an old bloke on a donkey, with emotional baggage and two children in tow.' Lizzie was and remains unbelievably good with my two daughters, Jasmine and Jessica. She took us all on right from the first meeting. Her kindness to us stands as a testimony of the grace and love God has poured into her, and her willingness to serve and love others first.

So as well as bringing Christ into my life, Paul also introduced me to my beautiful and wonderful wife to be!

I asked Paul Hubbard to give his impressions of what he has experienced with us through these times. Paul was the man who brought me to the Lord and who was by my side over the first eleven years of my walk with God and the first seven years of the CAP story.

Paul's Story

'When I first met John, he didn't know the Lord and had no knowledge of his ways, workings or wonders. For some inexplicable reason (at least to John), he not only rented his house to us, he also partly furnished it which was a miracle since we had just arrived from Norway with no home, no money and very few personal possessions.

We settled in and over the next few months were able to spend time with him, gently opening him up to the good news of what Jesus had done for him. It was not long before he had given over his life to the goodness and mercy of God, and his life began to be dramatically affected. It is true to say that although those early years were painful, perhaps even traumatic, they were also blessed.

Here was a man who had been steeped in the ways of the world, had been caught up in the 'rat race' and perhaps viewed by many as successful. There is no doubt that God had given John a mega-sized gift. But as he came to know the power of God at work in his life and faced his life and motives in the environment of God's Word, love and compassion, the journey of transformation began to take place.

I have of course many memories of that journey so far, both of John and of what has become a wonderful life-transforming ministry and charity.

One of my most treasured memories is early on in the beginning of the ministry, when perhaps only the two of us were around. It was a particularly difficult and distressing situation; John had gone to court on behalf of and with a client. He had done everything he could. He had used all his God-given ability and gifting to save this couple from losing their home. I had remained at John's house in prayer. When John arrived I knew it had been painful and upsetting. He had no words to communicate what was going on in his heart or to express the grief and depth of compassion he felt. We wept, it was all we could do.

It was at this moment I felt the love, compassion and goodness of God being birthed in the ministry. This is still very evident today but in greater measure; a stream that flows; a foundation to build upon. The above situation has been replayed in different ways many times over throughout CAP's history.

My own tribute to John and to the Lord – who has so marvellously created, loved and developed him and continues to do so – is that he is a man of compassion, vision, passion and evangelism. The message about Jesus has become a living reality, which he not only hears, but hears with faith. This faith leads him to action, even in the midst of personal circumstances which in many other lives would disable and hinder.

For John, Christianity is a reality; full of possibilities and adventure. May it be that for you too!'

Paul Hubbard
Former Trustee, Christians Against Poverty

CHAPTER THREE

CHRISTIANS AGAINST POVERTY IS BORN!

It was all starting to look very good again on the outside by 1996. I had a large beautiful home, was soon to be married and had a potentially lucrative financial future. I was due to become debt free within a couple of years, felt well-respected and was growing with God all the time. But I began to sense that I had a major decision to make. Either I continued to do it my way and really push for more 'success', or I put myself properly in God's hands and saw where he would take me.

I had only been a Christian for four years and for the first two I really struggled. When I look back it's amazing to see that despite my enormous shortfall as a young Christian and my lack of understanding, God moved very quickly when I decided to live the life he wanted. If you have been lukewarm for God for some time, don't be surprised how quickly he moves when you put him first.

Be encouraged if you have had difficulties and been away from God in a wilderness either brought on by circumstances, or your own mistakes, or any combination of the two. God is just a prayer and a decision away. He's ready, willing and able to restore all you may have lost.

As I pondered these thoughts in early March 1996, I realised that a window of opportunity was beginning to open. Within one year the department I was responsible for would begin to see a down turn in business and profits due to market changes. I didn't know what to do, but it occurred to me that this was a way to step out in faith and see if now was the time for God to begin releasing me. It was my first tentative step of faith. The truth is, I might not have taken this step had I known what the next few years were about to bring. Praise God for his wisdom in shielding me from this.

Feeling God was in control, on March 9, 1996 I rang my Managing Director, Ian Cummine, and told him we should consider shutting the department that I had built up. I explained that within a year the whole mortgage market would change and we would lose the commercial advantage we had enjoyed for four years.

Ian Cummine had been very influential in my career to that date. He was the first to really believe in me and he was always very generous in salaries and bonuses throughout my time working for him, which was about ten years in total in two stretches. He was a very sharp businessman and understood exactly what I was saying. He listened and said, 'Okay, we'll shut it then.' Twenty-one days later, I was made redundant. The department closed and business transferred. If I had wanted to stay on I'm sure he would have found a place for me. I did all this a few weeks before my annual bonus was due. However, Ian was very generous and paid my yearly bonus, something he didn't have to do. Again, God's favour is with the ones who will put their faith in him on the line. Looking back, I realised that God really honoured my integrity. With this pay out I was able to cover the costs of our forthcoming wedding and put the following year's maintenance on one side for my children.

Ian actually came to see me at CAP in October 2002 and I was able to thank him personally for how he had helped me at that very difficult time in my life, and for the very gracious and generous way he released me from working for him. He was stunned at what he saw and was very encouraging.

Encouraged by my first act of faith, I decided to take another step. I began to look at starting a Christian building society, finance company or bank. These sound like outrageous ideas, but with my background and experience they weren't totally unrealistic.

Then God broke in when I took a couple of days away with Paul Hubbard to attend a conference at Pilgrim Hall in East Sussex. It was a gathering of church leaders for teaching, rest and reflection. One morning I found myself in a queue for breakfast which went into two rooms, so I chose one. Then I randomly sat at one of eight tables and found myself next to a man I had never seen before or heard from since. I shared my ideas and they must have sounded very daft. He told me to ring a guy he knew called Nigel who was a venture capitalist and might be able to help me start either a bank or a building society. Out of the blue, God miraculously led me to the next phone call that was to prove one of the most important of my life.

On June 6, 1996, I rang Nigel. I found out he was neither a venture capitalist nor able to help with my request. Nevertheless, he did ask one of the most important questions anyone has ever asked me. He said, 'Why don't you see what you can do without needing anyone to help you start or any huge sum of money. What could you do on your own now?'

I went straight to my computer, I can't remember even praying. I just typed 'debt counselling.' This was it! I knew this was it. I could start now and get stuck in. I had found something I was qualified and able to do and I did not have to wait for anything.

Over the next six weeks leading up to our marriage, I spent a lot of time seeking God's heart for the poor, praying and studying the Bible. I designed a brochure, looked into money advice and just pressed ahead. We had nothing but debts and no real idea of what to do next. God had obviously put some entrepreneurial DNA within me that just said, 'Why not me? Why not now?' I registered the charity and was surprised no one else had registered the name Christians Against Poverty.

Lizzie and I got married on July 27, 1996. It was a most wonderful day and an example of God's grace in my life. Here I was with a beautiful Christian bride who loved me and wanted to be with me for the rest of her life whatever we would face. We were in a church with over a hundred of our friends, being married by Paul Hubbard, the man who had brought me to Christ and us together. Our God is truly awesome.

Less than a month after the big day, there was another! On August 22, 1996, Christians Against Poverty began. Just to put the record straight, Lizzie did know that I was about to start in full time ministry before we got married!

I still can't believe that Lizzie was up for what we actually did. There she was as a new bride, and we began our life together by getting rid of all our security and starting a Christian ministry with no money. I am eternally grateful for her faith in God and me, and for letting me just get on with what the Lord had called me to do. To this day she has never asked me to lay the work down or complained when things get tough.

We were all ready to go, armed with our first £10 gift and faith that God was with us. With a vision and a prayer we started. I posted off the brochure to eighty churches in Bradford and everyone I knew, asking more than four hundred people to support me. Then I simply sat back and waited for the cash and encouragement to flood in.

CHAPTER FOUR
CAP'S FIRST CLIENTS

Shock number one, 'This ministry thing can be hard.' We had this naive idea that everybody who heard of our vision, including the wider church, would be falling over themselves to support us in our step of faith. We felt sure they would rally to our vision and our needs. In fact, over the first six months only about fifteen people supported our work.

Then came shock number two, 'People who don't even know you will support you.' A lady called Janet who worked as a cashier at Lloyds bank noticed CAP's name on the paying-in book and asked for details of the work I was starting. This was the first time she had met me and to my utter amazement she sent £500 the next day. This kept us going for another month, what an encouragement! Then we received an anonymous gift of £500 and to this day I do not know who sent it. Two weeks later, the Church on the Way in Bradford sent CAP a £1,000 gift. It was astounding!

I wrote a simple brochure, sent it out to churches and gave it to friends. One of those friends, Angie, suggested CAP to my first two clients. In September 1996, armed with a note pad, calculator, enthusiasm and faith that God would help me, I went to see them.

My first two clients were Dennis and Denise. They were an ordinary couple living in an ex-council house. Denise was a school assistant and Dennis an auto-electrician. As soon as I sat down with Denise, the reality of what I was about to face over the coming years hit me. I listened as she explained how she had fallen into a spiral of borrowing to pay off debts, ever increasing interest payments and charges. She had reached a stage of total financial collapse and owed £24,000 to about ten companies. She was facing court action, possible eviction and the repossession of her house due to not paying their mortgage. If that wasn't enough, she then told me her husband had absolutely no idea about any of it.

I took a deep breath and thought, 'I know what to do in principle. I have spent seventeen years of my life preparing for this moment. I can do this.' Firstly, I tried to reassure her I could help, and that there was hope. The first thing I needed to do was explain things to her husband Dennis. She was distraught but agreed I should come back and tell him everything. I returned and with some fear and trepidation told Dennis the truth. I reiterated that although it looked impossible, I could get them out of the mess if they worked with me. He went into shock. Tears were streaming down his face. He didn't understand how they had got into this desperate situation. He just wanted to hear their home was safe, he wanted hope.

So, I started to work with them. The basic process remains the same to this day. It took me about three months and involved detailed negotiations with each creditor, getting them to accept reduced payments and to agree to stop charging any additional interest or add other charges. Dennis and Denise agreed not to borrow any more and to live within a budget. This meant that if they lived within their means, paid their disposable income to their creditors through CAP, and did not borrow any more money, they would be debt free in five years. Their mortgage and other priority payments such as gas, electricity and council tax including the agreed arrears repayment, would be paid first. This would stop any repossession action by the mortgage company. They were so grateful for the release of the pressure and simply did what they had agreed to do. The results were amazing and over the years it has been my privilege to see their circumstances change out of all recognition.

They saved up for years for their twenty-fifth wedding anniversary and went away for a cruise. In 2001, it was such a joy to see my very first clients totally debt free, in a new house and in charge of their money. That is what CAP is all about. It's about giving people a future hope and watching as their lives change before your eyes. Every month we see families come to the end of three, four and five year plans totally debt free and with their whole lives ahead of them. They are able to manage their finances, to save and not borrow. Dennis and Denise will always be the first couple who trusted CAP's way and they are an inspiration and encouragement to us all, and the thousands of families that have followed them over the years.

Denise with John, debt free, and having moved into a new home

Dennis and Denise's situation was fairly shocking but the next three months up to Christmas filled me with compassion time and time again. I saw things that really opened my eyes: families with hungry children, people in trauma having no hope, broken marriages, and the sheer havoc and distress financial difficulties bring about in people's lives. Their strife had a profound effect on me. They were what inspired me to drive CAP forward and see more people helped. It was strange that right from the first few weeks I knew I was born for this work and the thought of giving up never entered my mind. We had people who needed us. We simply had to carry on.

In the midst of all this, I was struggling with the way so many people responded so negatively to our work and vision. Christians berated me for, as they saw it, 'my lack of responsibility for my own family's needs.' Surely I should 'get a proper job and provide for my wife and children.' Other people thought because we lived in a nice house, that I had some sort of 'stash of cash.' How wrong could they have been! We were living from week to week, our mortgage was more than the house was worth and was beginning to go unpaid, and we were struggling with the remainder of our debts. Collection companies were threatening us with court action. Some people just blanked us. We could not understand why people were not willing to encourage and support us.

One particular letter caused me much distress and pain. Accusations were made against my personal integrity suggesting that my whole reason for starting CAP was for my own financial gain. I was accused of trying to make money out of the very people I was trying to help. All my efforts were utterly mocked and venomously attacked. Who did I think I was and what was I trying to achieve? Nothing I had done had amounted to much before so who was I trying to kid? Even my Christian faith was called into question and ridiculed.

I struggled with the tremendous sense of hurt and injustice at how I had been written off with such malice. Right when I was starting out, when I was vulnerable, weak in faith and wondering what I had done this rubbish had come through the letterbox.

This letter drew me to my old friend Nehemiah for the first time. In chapter six verse eight he had also received an open letter accusing him of false proclamations. Nehemiah simply says, 'Nothing like you are saying is happening; you are just making it up out of your head.'

Nehemiah's spirit said, I am not concerned with what you think. He just got on with it, he knew the truth and that God was with him.

After a few days of being very downhearted I can remember realising I could do nothing to vindicate myself. God knew and it was his opinion I was interested in, not what other people thought. I now see that I was starting the process of being released from the 'what other people think' syndrome. This is a disabling spirit that makes you bound to the opinions of others, rather than what God thinks and what you know is right.

Over the next two years problems with these people persisted, with accusations being levelled not just at me personally but questioning the integrity of the charity as a whole. They made accusations about our accounts and they even threatened to report us to the Charity Commission! At one stage Paul Hubbard, who was the chairman of the charity, wrote asking them to come and see for themselves the value of our work and to allay their fears. They never took him up on the offer and eventually fell silent.

The whole area of people not supporting or encouraging us is a difficult one. With the benefit of a little wisdom and maturity, I now realise that of course not everyone is going to get behind and support your dream. Many people are pursuing and supporting other visions. I was naive to expect everybody to support me.

Another difficulty was, and still is, explaining our philosophy of employing people rather than waiting for volunteers. All along CAP's main expense has been wages because we believe a worker is worth his wage like the Bible tells us. It would be unrealistic to expect the full-time commitment of such professional people if we asked them to volunteer. Mortgages have to be paid and lives have to be lived. If they are willing to work hard for us, stand in faith and give so much, it is our responsibility as a charity to make sure those needs are met. That's why we are so committed to paying good salaries and benefits.

I was still reeling from this hurtful letter when I met my second client. She came to me through a local vicar, the Rev Charles Barber, who I had met and sent some brochures to. A lady in his church was in great distress so he gave her the CAP brochure and suggested I could be of help.

Her name was Debbie Thompson. She was to become perhaps the most influential client CAP has ever had. I want to give you her story from my perspective and then Debbie will explain in her own words how CAP affected her life and where the Lord has brought her today.

I remember the day I walked into Debbie's house like it was yesterday. Her situation was as desperate as any I have seen. She was giving all her money to aggressive and manipulative collectors leaving her virtually nothing to feed her children with. She was within a few weeks of having her house repossessed and had spiralling debts. She had just a few pounds to feed her family for days and would make dumplings from nine pence bags of flour and buy tins of beans or spaghetti to feed her two sons.

She told me how, when working as an auxiliary nurse, she would go to work with no food and just enough bus fare to get home because she had given all of her wage to satisfy debt collectors. She described how when the 'hat' went round for gifts for her work friends who were leaving or getting married, she would have to go into the toilet to avoid the embarrassment of not having fifty pence to put in. She knew that people used to say behind her back that she was stingy, yet Debbie is one of the most generous people you could ever meet.

Being in debt can be a private hell with no escape; it is an ever increasing torment and hardship. Debbie's case, together with another lady who was near to suicide when I went to see her, were the ones that really got me determined to make CAP grow and succeed. I became desperate to see thousands of other families released from such oppression and hopelessness into a future with God.

She was such a gentle lady, full of honour, yet broken and with no hope. I completed a financial statement and basically got stuck in with her creditors. I eventually got them to agree to reduced payments, stabilised the finances and Debbie and her family began to live a decent life.

Debbie has become a legend of CAP and contributed so much to the charity. In 1998 she became a Trustee and served for ten years.

In October 2002, Debbie was employed as our National Prayer Co-ordinator. As well as co-ordinating prayer, Debbie also acted as pastoral support to our staff and sat on the International Trustee Board. She has gone from being suicidal in 1996, with the possibility of losing her home, to woman who God has used mightily for the benefit of others.

Debbie's Story

'Things seemed to be going pretty well, we had our own home and a successful driving school. When our first son was born it all seemed great. Looking back, I can see that we were quite complacent about money, we didn't think ahead or plan for any problems.

The problems started when I was pregnant with my second son, nothing too major just some health problems that meant I had to work less. However, winter was a slow period for the driving school and it never fully picked up again. There was a car crash and in just a short time things were falling apart. I was used to a certain amount of money coming in and it didn't seem a worry to take out credit. What I had I considered normal, a three piece suite, a fridge from a local store, clothes from a catalogue. I always thought we could pay it back. But now we were juggling payments and missing things – including the mortgage. Things just spiralled. We tried to sell the house before it was repossessed but were a couple of weeks short of the sale going through when they took it.

My husband decided to try running a shop, which we could live above, and also keep the driving school going. I went back to nursing on nights. The shop wasn't a good idea and increased the debts rather than paying them off. It was in a bad part of town with terrible living conditions. The pressure was increasing and we were all struggling. After a year of living like this I went to my parents, I just couldn't see my children in that situation any longer. I said to my husband that we could start again somewhere else when he was ready.

While at my mum's I had time to take stock and couldn't believe the mess we were in. I would regularly think about killing myself but couldn't bear to leave my sons. I had always believed in the existence of God but not really taken much notice! But in desperation I started to pray. I asked God to get us back together as a family, promising that, if he did, I would stop messing about and go to church and follow him. We did get a house and I did start to go to church. I gave my life to God, went on an Alpha course and really committed myself to it.

We had six months or so of peace and enjoying being together, then the debts starting catching up from the driving school and shop.

Phone calls were constantly coming from people we owed money to, and letters threatening court action. I was trying to keep people happy but it was impossible. The pressure was terrible. I think I lost the plot in the middle of it all. I would hide away at work if there were collections for presents for people. Not being able to give was so hard. Not going on nights out and having to try to come up with plausible excuses was so depressing.

Shopping times were like military manoeuvres, trying to wring out the most from the money available. It was a regular thing to go and buy beans, oil and flour, and eat dumplings and beans. This was really stodgy food, no nutritional value but you feel full. Trips out were off limits, clothes were not on the agenda. I remember shouting really badly at my son when he came home from school having put his knee through his new school trousers.

It's hard to understand now but I was paying as much money as possible to our creditors, so much that we often had no food. I remember being sat at home with no food at all, we had nothing. I asked God to do something before the kids got home from school. The kids ran in from school all excited asking if they could go to my neighbour Pauline's for tea. She didn't know what an answer to my prayers that was.

All this was hidden from people of course. There was so much guilt and shame involved. Sometimes my eldest sister would take me shopping and fill up the trolley with food, which was wonderful. I know she did it for the children, but I was so ashamed.

Eventually I told my vicar and he gave me the leaflet for CAP. I telephoned John Kirkby in September 1996 in tears, absolutely desperate. My husband was on the verge of leaving but he stayed, and John just blew our socks off. He didn't judge but just offered a helping hand. He came the next day and for the first time we looked at the whole situation.

John worked out a budget for us. He gave us a simple account book and showed me how to balance all our essential living costs including the luxury of weekly food money! He also spoke to all our creditors and arranged a repayment plan that we could maintain. Within a very short space of time our lives changed dramatically. No more picking the phone up with that awful sinking feeling, no more dreading the postman!

Unfortunately, in 2000 my husband did leave us. Our debts were not fully repaid and with him no longer involved I had to leave my job and go bankrupt. 2001 was not a great year with the divorce and bankruptcy. As you can imagine I was devastated. I lost my home again, my job, and single parenthood was overwhelming at times. I was exhausted, but God has been so present in our lives. He kept me moving forward.

In 1998, CAP's management board asked me to represent the clients as a Trustee of the charity and I accepted. I could see that thousands of people needed this help and the vision of centres in every town really caught me. Then, in 2002 I was asked to lead prayer for CAP – God is funny isn't he! I wouldn't have picked me but I guess a lot of us might say that. The team believed someone needed to head up prayer so that it didn't lose focus as we grew. I became National Prayer Co-ordinator and had an important pastoral role among the staff. Then in May 2006, I was blown away when John asked me to sit on the International Board to ensure that prayer remains a major part of CAP's international work.

Debbie, who is now debt free

With God we have gone from strength to strength. Now we have a lovely home in a cosy terrace house, I have a great job and I have no debts! It's a privilege to have been part of something that is such a practical expression of God's heart. Certainly there are bad days when the past comes to haunt me, but this is happening less and less.

The most precious thing to be restored is my relationship with my sons. I let them down badly for a long time and it could have ruined our relationship forever, but praise God and because of God, we are very close. We have talked through the past and I have apologised. I am so grateful for the last few years where I have been able to show I can be a good mum and look after them well. They are both Christians and have experienced what God can do and who he is. One example of how things are so much better – the other day my son brought four friends round to the house after a basketball match and they proceeded to make bacon sandwiches. They were in the fridge, in the biscuit tin, sitting round the kitchen table eating and chatting away – it was fantastic! I am just so thankful that I didn't have to care that they nearly emptied my kitchen cupboards!

I want to say a massive thank you on behalf of all clients past, present and future to anybody who has ever supported CAP through prayer or finance. You really have no idea what you have done, but one day God will say, 'Well done, my true and faithful servant.' You may well meet clients in heaven who would not have been there without your faithful heart to CAP.'

Debbie Thompson
Second-ever CAP client

CHAPTER FIVE

GOD SPEAKS: 'DO NOT BE DISCOURAGED'

JANUARY TO JULY 1997

As 1996 drew to an end I started writing my diary to keep a record just between me and God of my daily struggles, never for one minute thinking anyone else would ever read it. It was only years later, as I began to read small extracts when preaching, that I was encouraged that the story should be told. These diary entries give you a very raw account of how tough things were in the early days and they stand as a testament to God's faithfulness. I'm pleased to say that things aren't quite so traumatic now, but occasionally we're still hit by the same lack of support and encouragement. The challenge remains to continue to trust in God and step out in faith when he calls us to something. Throughout the history of CAP, God has showed himself faithful time and again, and these pages speak of that.

December 31, 1996

As I look out from my bedroom office at home over a very snowy and cold Bradford, I am somehow overcome by many feelings and thoughts. What does 1997 hold for us? How will we cope emotionally and financially? What will happen to CAP?

43

These are just a few of my concerns as I look forward into 1997. I always think it is important to state where we are and what difficulties we face. It helps me put things into perspective and shows me how hopeless my circumstances would be were it not for the Lord working in every area of my life. It also helps to remind me that without his grace, guidance and provision I would be nowhere.

Our personal situation is very difficult. We are two and a half months behind with our mortgage. Although the building society has been understanding, we know that if, by April this year, we are unable to have some possibility of maintaining the mortgage payments, we will be forced to sell the house. I bought it back in 1989 for £125,000 and I have tried to sell it twice with no success. It is probably worth less than the mortgage, which is £112,000 with interest being added and a monthly payment of £800. Losing the house is something I have faced before and although it would be a traumatic event the most important thing for me would be that I could see that the Lord moved us on, not that we lost the house. I am also very concerned how my wonderful wife Lizzie and in particular my two girls Jasmine and Jessica would cope with the loss of their home. We need another £800 per month just to pay the bills and remaining debts. Where will this income of £1,600 per month come from?

I am also very disappointed and upset at the lack of support we have received for the charity. In real terms, it is our only source of income other than Lizzie's small wage, which just feeds us each month. We only have a guaranteed monthly income of £155 and we have just sent 500 newsletters out before Christmas. As yet, the response has been very small. So many people seem oblivious to our plight and seem unable to give us even the smallest amount of financial support. These are people who have known us for years, Christians and non-Christians who seem unable to even ask us how we are managing or how the work is going. I need God's grace and understanding towards this. Both of us take this lack of interest so hard. We have written to more than 80 churches in the Bradford area and only two churches have supported us: my home church, Christian Life Church and Church on the Way. We were astonished though by the financial support we received from one Church of England vicar. I have written to more than 100 large companies in Bradford asking for some support and only two have offered any help: Empire Stores and Seabrook Crisps. Only about 15 people have helped; if only they knew how much it means to us.

Four such people spring to mind: Charles Barber, Janet Green, Derek Gardiner and Olga Pochibko. These four people don't really know us, had not even met us and knew nothing of our true plight, but have supported us. We pray they will know just how much it has meant to us and it is through their actions and people like them that the Lord has confirmed his commitment to us. However, with such an overall weight of problems, why do we carry on? There are only two reasons. The first is for the people who we are helping through CAP. I only have to look at the files and think of the people to know that what we are doing is right from the Lord's heart.

Each one was in a desperate situation of real oppression and poverty and just to think of individuals being able to buy food for their children, still having a roof over their heads and relationships being touched by the Lord is reason enough to keep going. Any price we have to pay is bearable just to know that people are being helped. When I look out of my window over Bradford I know that there are hundreds if not thousands of other families who right now are suffering poverty and oppression through debt. If we can help one hundred families in 1997 then let all the honour, praise and glory go to God. This brings me on to the second and most important reason to carry on; I believe with all my heart that this is God's will.

I have just spent this morning re-reading some of the scriptures that the Lord has laid on my heart for CAP and for continuing:

'Speak up for those who cannot speak for themselves, for the rights of all who are destitute. Speak up and judge fairly; defend the rights of the poor and needy.'

(Proverbs 31:8–9)

'You have been a refuge for the poor, a refuge for the needy in his distress, a shelter from the storm and a shade from the heat. For the breath of the ruthless is like a storm driving against a wall and like the heat of the desert.'

(Isaiah 25:4)

'The Spirit of the Lord is on me, because he has anointed me to preach good news to the poor. He has sent me to proclaim freedom for the prisoners and recovery of sight for the blind, to release the oppressed, to proclaim the year of the Lord's favour.'

(Luke 4:18–19)

. . . 'Be strong and courageous, and do the work. Do not be afraid or discouraged, for the Lord God, my God, is with you. He will not fail you or forsake you until all the work for the service of the temple of the Lord is finished . . .'

(I Chronicles 28:20; given to me 6 September 1996)

'Therefore, since we have been justified through faith, we have peace with God through our Lord Jesus Christ, through whom we have gained access by faith into this grace in which we now stand. And we rejoice in the hope of the glory of God. Not only so, but we also rejoice in our sufferings, because we know that suffering produces perseverance; perseverance, character; and character, hope. And hope does not disappoint

us, because God has poured out his love into our hearts by the Holy Spirit, whom he has given us.'

(Romans 5:1–5; given to me 19 September 1996)

'Consider it pure joy, my brothers, whenever you face trials of many kinds, because you know that the testing of your faith develops perseverance. Perseverance must finish its work so that you may be mature and complete, not lacking anything. If any of you lacks wisdom, he should ask God, who gives generously to all without finding fault, and it will be given to him. But when he asks, he must believe and not doubt, because he who doubts is like a wave of the sea, blown and tossed by the wind. That man should not think he will receive anything from the Lord; he is a double-minded man, unstable in all he does.

The brother in humble circumstances ought to take pride in his high position. But the one who is rich should take pride in his low position, because he will pass away like a wild flower. For the sun rises with scorching heat and withers the plant; its blossom falls and its beauty is destroyed. In the same way, the rich man will fade away even while he goes about his business.

Blessed is the man who perseveres under trial, because when he has stood the test, he will receive the crown of life that God has promised to those who love him."

(James 1:2–12; given to me 19 September 1996)

When I re-read these wonderful words of encouragement, they are almost the last word for all of us in CAP. In 1 Chronicles it describes David's attitude:

'The Jebusites who lived there said to David "You will not get in here'. Nevertheless, David captured the fortress of Zion, the city of David."'

(1 Chronicles 11:4b–5)

He must have understood God's heart and decided to carry on. It was the same for us: that 'nevertheless' attitude only comes from knowing God is with you.

The word of God has both sustained us and encouraged us. I would often spend time with him asking for advice and encouragement. I would read daily devotionals and listen to other preachers. Whenever I felt in my spirit that a word was specifically for me or CAP, I noted it.

The words of encouragement I received through the Bible stand as a testimony to God's amazing grace. Without his faithfulness and miraculous provision in terms of strength, determination and the sheer will to go on, we would have crumbled.

January 22, 1997

This weekend's sponsored walk along the canal at Shipley was a real example of something we are beginning to realise is to be an ongoing battle. How will we cope with a lack of support?

Not one of the 14 people who we are helping came to the walk, rang to see how it went or even raised any sponsorship, however small. I found this very difficult as I have given so much into each situation, and I expected some help. However, as always, it revealed something I needed and will always need to deal with and that is, 'do I help people expecting them to understand the cost I pay and respond, or do I do it because it is right, and the Lord has called me to help?' This has been a very interesting time and of course I have had to reaffirm that my calling is to help people irrespective of whether they appreciate it. I want to help them and show them God's love.

On the other hand, I was so encouraged by a friend named Paul Cribb who ran the whole way and raised £100; and Sheila, a brand new member of our Church, walked and raised some money. Steven and Karen Mason brought their two sons and walked all the way.

We also sent out 250 letters regarding the 'Awareness Evening' and asked for more regular support. Again, only one person responded with some regular sponsorship and nothing from so many people. I now feel that I don't need to beg any more and that if people don't want to support us then that's fine and I should not put any more pressure on them. A few more people have come forward after our awareness evening which over 30 people attended. We now have two more regular givers and another two on the way.

We now call our regular givers 'Life Changers' and it's interesting to note that despite very little encouragement, I somehow knew that it was right to just keep asking and to develop regular individual financial support. God bless every one who has sown into the ministry. Every pound has encouraged us and still does. It keeps us sharp in terms of making sure our work is relevant to people and that they are prepared to continue to support us. Please consider joining us by becoming a 'Life Changer' today![1]

January 22, 1997 continued

The last two days have been some of the most traumatic so far regarding our financial situation. My attempts to come to agreements with my creditors have become more and more difficult. Our financial situation is this; in three months we will need an income of £1600 per month to stay in our house, keep up my debt payments and pay our bills.

While praying this morning and feeling I was at the end of my ability to cope, the phone rang. It was Angela Spencer from

---

1   There are 'Life Changer' forms at the back of the book!

church. She rang simply to say God had told her to ring and that I
should not give up, and to read Joshua,

*'Have I not commanded you? Be strong and courageous.
Do not be terrified, do not be discouraged, for the Lord your
God will be with you wherever you go.'*

(Joshua 1:9)

I also read the following in Matthew.

*'Therefore everyone who hears these words of mine and
puts them into practice is like a wise man who built his
house on the rock. The rain came down, the streams rose,
and the winds blew and beat against the house; yet it did
not fall because it had its foundations on the rock.'*

(Matthew 7:24-25)

To be honest, the wind is stronger than I had expected, the waves
are bigger and more powerful and I am weaker than I had hoped.
But I know we are built upon 'The Rock' and as his word says,
'Yet it did not fall, because it had its foundation on the rock.'

My friend Paul Hubbard came this morning and we were able
to pray and believe that the Lord was in control and that I had a
job to do. I was lifted in faith. I am determined to continue.

Paul has been there for me so many times over the years. He has always
been able to stand with me to express his faith in God, in me and that
we will get through. He probably has no idea just how grateful we have
been so many times for his encouragement and commitment to us. He
is so strong in the Lord and the Word. He is a wonderful man of God
and I consider myself privileged to know him.

January 28, 1997

Over the weekend the building society called and stated that
they would not accept my request for a couple of months to try
and sort things out, and they would start proceedings and action
to protect their interests. After much prayer we decided that
today we would put our wonderful house up for sale. We are

three months behind with our mortgage. We believe that God will provide for us but if he has any other ideas or plans then we want to remain open. I will put a sign up in faith that if God wants to keep us in this house he is big enough to do it and provide the money in time.

I feel a bit like Abraham when God said sacrifice your son. I am not suggesting that I would be able to do anything which remotely resembled that act of faith, but I feel that by giving my wife, children, house, reputation and life into the Lord's hands I am left with nothing but the Lord.

It's times like this that you are tempted and really wonder what is happening to you. A credit card company who I still owe money to, rang up and simply said, 'Give us our money!' No compassion, only insults and suggestions that I should go and get a proper job. Income Support said unless I was prepared to sign a contract stating I would seek alternative employment then they would not help us in any way. I can't lie just to get money, my God is bigger than that.

My wonderful wife is beside me and I feel so much for her facing our first year of marriage with an uncertain future, not knowing where we might end up. Her support and belief in me is beyond my understanding.

Two people touched me today in all the difficulties. Firstly my friend Avril said we could stay in her caravan in the garden if we lost the house. Her compassion for us was unbelievable. It has only just sunk in that homelessness is a possibility. Am I prepared to put my words and faith into action and continue with CAP and the ministry work if that is the price we have to pay?

Secondly, two of our friends and supporters, Chris and Mark, said they would make a monthly donation. They believe in us and know our situation.

I have been thinking of my overall situation. My children are asleep upstairs, Lizzie is out and I have wept in my office. When I think about our circumstances and of what we might have to go through, I can feel myself saying, 'No Lord, this is just too much to take.'

What can I say? I am a broken man. All the rejection, the lack of support, the relentless pressure and uncertainty seems too much to bear.

Yet I just have to think of Dennis and Denise, Debbie Thompson, Carl and many of the people I have helped and will help. I know I have no option but to carry on. Something deep within me says, 'this is the way son, trust me, I will not let you down. I understand your tears and fears and I will store them up for my future glory.' I am trying to be strong as Joshua was commanded but I am falling short. I need the Lord more now than at any time in my life. I have nothing else to hold on to.

I must carry on. People need me tomorrow. I have a funding document to complete, a life to live and a wife and children who need me. I pray that the Lord will meet me just where I am in this situation of destitution and need. I know he will and that somehow he will find a way in the darkness. Over recent weeks I have been going to Church on the Way in Bradford to listen to Charles Price. He is a great Bible teacher and has been speaking on 'Treasures in the Darkness'. To be honest, it feels like it doesn't get much darker than this and I just know that there are treasures as yet unseen in this darkness. Praise God.

February 26, 1997

What a month! Over the last four weeks I have been totally consumed with completing our funding document and our new promotional video with a good friend, Malcolm West. Last Friday I completed a mailshot letting people know what we are doing. The situation is now as they say, on the edge! We face a very desperate financial situation. All the money that CAP has, and some it doesn't even have has been swallowed up with the £1,000 cost of the funding document. This has meant that I have only received £200 over the last eight weeks, and it went towards my mortgage.

I have basically reached the end of the road financially, with four months arrears on my mortgage, £400 needed in the next week for bills and debts with virtually nothing left.

A promised £750 gift has not come in and I just don't know which way to turn. Yet again, I am faced with the reality that many people just don't understand or are not sufficiently moved to help. Although we have another two supporters, we only have a total regular monthly income of £275.

When I sit and think over the last year since I left my job, I can sense the enemy pulling on my emotions saying that people don't believe in me. For instance only five people attended my seminar last night. One person whom I am helping and who faces enormous problems rang up and said they were a 'bit tired' so wouldn't be coming. I was a 'bit tired' - I had worked since 8am and would not finish until 11pm. Will this constant and unbelievable pressure on my finances ever go away? Am I destined to a life of unsupported ministry?

Can I carry on paying the price if CAP is destined to remain small and we are only going to help a small number of people? If I am to have my house repossessed and be destitute and in debt for the rest of my life, would I carry on? The honest answer is that I don't feel that I could do that. The reasons are partly my lack of faith in my ability to sustain how I live for a long period of time, but secondly, I know that my God will not allow that to happen. When absolutely nothing you can see confirms what the Lord has said to you, you are left only with his word and promises.

I believe that the Lord will provide for us, that we will not live a destitute life, that my debts will be cleared and that CAP will grow to be a wonderful ministry helping thousands of people. I see a time when we will be blessed financially and I will have a reasonable income and be able to afford to live, pay my bills and have a decent life for my wife and children. I can feel my spirits lifted by simply writing these truths down, and the enemy has no defence against the promises of God.

All I have to do is carry on – that's my responsibility. The rest is up to God. I am left not knowing what will happen but knowing God cares and it will be him who sees us through, supports us, encourages us and ultimately provides for our needs.

April 11, 1997

Over the last six weeks, things have really got going as far as the ministry is concerned. We are now taking on about one or two new families per week and the results are incredible. People are becoming Christians and it is a real honour and privilege to see how God is using me to minister his grace, love and compassion.

As far as finances and funding are concerned, we have had the best month ever in March. Nearly £2,000 came in and I got paid enough to actually put something towards my mortgage. I have just read Loren Cunningham's book 'Living on the Edge,' and it has been a revelation to me. He was the one who started YWAM (Youth With A Mission). He never gave up. God eventually met all his needs supernaturally and grew the ministry into the world-wide organisation it is today.

Loren Cunningham's book was a great source of encouragement to me and it was one of the motivations for me to write 'Nevertheless.' My hope is that someone starting out in ministry may one day read this book and if they are even half as encouraged, challenged and inspired as I was with 'Living on the Edge,' then that will be wonderful.

April 11, 1997 continued

I have had several tempting opportunities that would have allowed me to get my finances back under control. One was a part-time job and the other was the idea of commercially using the services and products we have developed to make money. I felt a little uneasy, and I have had it confirmed by a recent trustee meeting that God is in control, not me. The ministry work is more than full time and that's where God wants me. If I went down these new avenues I would only try to take back control instead of believing in his provision.

Our personal circumstances continue to get worse. As far as our home is concerned, we received the dreaded letter from the building society saying the account was to be transferred to the collection and recovery department (i.e. repossession action was to be started). Both Lizzie and myself are strangely calm about it all. We realise that God doesn't need a letter from the building society to tell him how much arrears we are in. His plans and purposes are not suddenly altered by a letter.

Having said that, someone is coming to view our beautiful house tomorrow. All the concern about where we might live and whether we are really going to be asked to give up our home, suddenly becomes a reality.

Today I was introduced to David Evans from Tearfund. They are a huge international Christian relief agency working mainly in developing countries who might be able to help with funding. I find myself wondering what God is trying to tell me. Why am I unable to pay the mortgage? Why doesn't anybody just send us a cheque for £10,000? William Spencer (who was volunteering for me one day a week), got a great deal of insight into this 'wilderness experience' we are going through. He felt the Lord say,

> *'A seed which receives no water will only survive if it sends its root deep underground trying to find the water. The eventual tree that results is strong and fully able to use the rains when they come. God needs to ensure that we will be able to manage what he has for us.'*

I get a sense that I need to just rest in his arms and stop trying to work it out. I must rest in the certain knowledge that all things work to the good of those who love the Lord. I am also reminded of Matthew 6:25–34 that tells us not to worry. At the end it says,

'Seek first his kingdom and righteousness and all these things will be given to you as well.'

I pray that God will help me to keep my eyes focused on him, as I would surely sink if I looked at my circumstances and the fact that it all seems impossible. It's a bit like the Apostle Peter, when he walked on the water then sank when he took his eyes off Jesus. I also realise that as he sank, Jesus held him and he was safe.

April 29, 1997

A very good day with David Evans from Tearfund yesterday. He was very impressed by our work and I took him to see three of the people I am helping. He can't guarantee anything but there is hope that they may be able to fund us with up to £10,000! We won't know until about the end of May but praise God for a small breakthrough.

I had a call from the building society today as well, and if we don't get the funding before the end of May they have no option but to begin the process of repossessing our home. I feel strangely calm. It looks as if the Lord is either going to take us to the wire or he has somewhere else for us to live. It's at times like this when my mind works overtime wondering what will come next and how we will cope. Am I missing something? Is there anything else I could do?

I have often spoken out that we were prepared to pay the price of our financial security and our home. It's all so easy to say, but what a difference when it looms before you as a reality. It really tests your faith and belief in what you are doing. All the old chestnuts of not understanding people's lack of support have surfaced all over again. Should we share our plight? Is there any point in us continuing the fight for our home?

The uncertainty is killing me. If only I knew, I could begin to plan but the Lord obviously has a reason for this uncertainty. If he wants to know if I am serious, he surely must realise that I will give my life for him and the vision he has given me. I know he knows that, so why the test? Why the wait? Why the anguish?

I have just read Psalm 91. What a word!

'I will say of the Lord: "He is my refuge and my fortress, my God, in whom I trust."'

'He will cover you with his feathers and under his wing you will find refuge, his faithfulness will be your shield and rampart.'

'"Because he loves me," says the Lord, "I will rescue him; I will protect him, for he acknowledges my name. He will call upon me and I will answer him. I will be with him in trouble, I will deliver him and honour him."'

(Psalm 91:2, 4, 14-15)

Praise God for his word just in time! I know that I was born for such a time as this. This ministry is God's work. It is right out of his Word. He will sustain me, he will uphold us because the Bible says so. I have nothing else to hang on to except his word and I will not let go of the calling or his promises.

I hope the following extract will bring home to you what it feels like when you owe someone money and they are constantly wanting more and you have no more to give. I had debts from my past and had arranged with each creditor except one to accept reduced monthly payments. One company refused to understand and they had continued to hassle me. I was reaching breaking point. It's these types of experiences that the Lord has used to give me a real compassion and drive to help the many thousands of people who face the same situations.

May 3, 1997

10.30am

Yesterday morning, Saturday, just as we were setting off for a day out with the girls, the phone rang. It was the same credit card collection company. The lady on the other end of the phone simply carried on where they left off last time they spoke to me and she simply demanded more money. As I explained my plight,

at the end of each exchange she simply stated that £10 per
month was not enough. I explained I was on a very low income,
not eligible for any benefit and had been paying without missing
for five years. Even when I explained that I was facing losing my
home over the next few weeks, had no regular income, that I was
running a Christian charity working to help the poor she simply
said: 'More money or we will take you to court!'

It is important to understand that having worked in the finance
industry for seventeen years, I know that the company would
get nothing if they took me to court. I know I have been totally
honourable in all my financial affairs. However, this lady made
me feel like dirt! Not for the first time throughout the last five
years her attitude and threats almost brought me to my knees.
What was I supposed to do? I have to admit I finally lost it. I
just could not talk to this lady, and the feelings of helplessness,
injustice and vulnerability were too much to bear. I had to ask her
to ring me on Tuesday when I would be able to talk better and I
have to admit I put the phone down.

I am not a man who can't fight his corner, but she finally
ground me down so much that I basically cracked. After the
telephone conversation I could hardly speak to Lizzie, and she
was unwell. She suffers from some sort of stomach problem,
where every so often she is physically sick for about two days.
The doctors don't know what it is even though she has had it
investigated. However, she knew what pain, utter desperation
and dejection I felt. Somehow we were able to pick ourselves up
and go for a day out with some wonderful Christian friends, Chris
and Mark, who paid for our day out at Harewood House.

Throughout the day I kept feeling so down about everything.
I alone know the true extent of our financial situation. We need
£250 over the next week to keep going. The Lord was so good to
me. He picked me up and somehow we had a great day - I hope

none of the friends who were with us would have known how I was feeling.

Today, Sunday, Lizzie is unwell again and although I try to keep her aware of what is happening I don't burden her if I feel nothing would be helped by her worrying as well.

The 'Word For Today' for the last three days has been a great source of encouragement for me. Friday's word was 'Patience is the bridge that carries you from the will of God to the promises of God.' It went on 'If you do the will of God on this side, the promises are waiting for you on the other.' The key point was this, 'Bridges come in different lengths and only God knows how long they are.' The question asked was 'Are you doing the will of God?' I have to say, as far as I am aware, we are doing the will of God.

The second question was, 'Are you walking patiently and confidently before the Lord in this matter?' I am convinced that we are on a bridge with a definite and glorious end. I don't know how long it is or how rough it will get, but I know with God's help and the faith he has given me, we will get to the other side. I just pray it's not too long and we will still be around to enjoy the other side.

I feel so overwhelmed by the size of my problems and the magnitude by which things are out of my control. I am a practical man, a man who has not relied on anyone, someone who is willing to give his all for what he believes. However, I have never realised just how insignificant I am against my situation and problems. I am doing what I can, I continue to serve and be faithful in the small things.

'But God chose the foolish things of the world to shame the wise; God chose the weak things of the world to shame the strong.'

(I Corinthians 1:27)

I have decided that I am going to use all the God-given gifts I have to take on this credit card collection company. I will start on Tuesday at the local county court to see if I can, with the

Lord's guidance and help, take these people to court and see if I can win justice for my case. In the long run it would also create a precedent where companies will be forced to accept a reasonable and just offer of debt repayment. I can imagine what the result of that would bring in the work we undertake. I am encouraged by many proverbs that speak of the Lord helping and supporting the lowly in court.

> *'Do not exploit the poor because they are poor and do not crush the needy in court, for the Lord will take up their case and will plunder those who plunder them.'*
>
> *(Proverbs 22:22)*

> *'Better to be lowly in spirit and among the oppressed than to share plunder with the proud.'*
>
> *(Proverbs 16:19)*

> *'He who mocks the poor shows contempt for their Maker; whoever gloats over disaster will not go unpunished.'*
>
> *(Proverbs 17:5)*

Although I did not know it, this was the start of CAP's insolvency service. This desperate five-year battle with this debt collection company would eventually give me the knowledge to help other people facing huge debt. Only God could use such circumstances for good. We now have a specialist insolvency service, which has helped hundreds of families facing similar insurmountable repayment of debt.

May 10, 1997

Today is an example of the different set of emotions that I face on a daily basis. First of all, my insecurities and weaknesses have been exposed by the way both Lizzie and myself are pulling apart rather than together in our situations. We got into a real state over what I should wear at a friends wedding. It wiped me out all last night and then again this morning.

Then I opened the mail and got £500 from the 'William Brooke Benevolent Fund,' praise God! Then the very next letter

was from the building society refusing my totally in faith offer on
my mortgage. They are giving me 14 days or they will pass my
account to collection and recoveries. The next letter was from
Tearfund saying it would take about two months before anything
could be arranged. My great hope of immediate financial support
is gone. The pressure of the ministry workload I face is great and
I am just falling behind all the time. I feel very lonely and isolated,
as if by choice I have shut myself away and I have virtually
closed down.

Praise God that I have him to fall back on. He knows my
needs, he has provided the essential requirements like food and
he will continue to provide. Why no future financial resource?
I feel like one of the three lepers in 2 Kings 7. They were outside
the gates of Samaria in a desert. Inside the city there was a great
famine, people were eating their own children and spending
thousands of pounds on a donkey head to eat! These lepers
were outcasts from their own people and as they looked round
they were surrounded by the army of Ben-Hadad which had laid
siege to Samaria.

*'Why stay here until we die? If we say, "We'll go into the city"
– the famine is there, and we will die. And if we stay here, we
will die. So let us go over to the camp of the Arameans and
surrender. If they spare us, we live, if they kill us we die.'*
(2 Kings 7:3-4)

I feel like those lepers; every way I can go looks like certain
death. If I give up, I'm finished. If I stop, I'm finished. I only
have one option and that is to carry on, and if I fail, I will fail
trying and if I'm finished then so be it. I've nearly had enough.
'Nevertheless' I will just carry on whatever.

I am encouraged that God went ahead of the lepers and
performed miracles before their very eyes and the army fled and
they just could not believe what they found in the enemy camp an
abundance for themselves. They immediately relieved the siege
of Samaria and all the people were released from the famine.
There are many parallels with my situation but I can't yet see the

miracles. However, I know that God goes before me and my only task is to keep going forward with his calling and know that God is with me.

Our first year ended, and what a year it had been. We had got the charity up and running and we had proved that we could change lives. People were becoming Christians! It had been a massive test and struggle but we were as convinced as ever that we were on the right track. We had seen thirty-nine families and had a total income of just £10,413, but we were under way. What would the second year hold for us all?

It is strange to read of this almost unexplainable confidence and expectant faith God had given me. I obviously knew that everything was going to be all right. It is also obvious to me that at this very dark time I had the grace of God for what I was facing. I was about three months early in my timing and a few thousand pounds out but there was a sense from deep within me that something was about to break. Praise God for his grace when we need it most.

June 1, 1997

We are waiting to hear whether our house will be repossessed. We have just survived the last three weeks on a gift from someone I really did not expect to give us anything.

It's strange what things cause me difficulties, it's not the big things, but the little things. Like not being able to get the picture frame I wanted for one of my paintings. Yet we manage every week. It's the constant need and uncertainty that tends to grind you down. As soon as one thing is paid, another is due. You constantly have no knowledge of where it will come from. Next week is a great example. We need some money for petrol and a day out with the children tomorrow, let's say £30. We still owe £30 for Lizzie's bridesmaid dress, £50 for next weekend, £90 to pay the bills by the 10th, £140 for our debt repayments by the 15th and then the mortgage. Currently we have virtually nothing either in any bank or our house. We have been here many times.

I have been getting a sense that God is about to open up
the floodgates and provision is about to flow. Joshua and the
miraculous crossing of the Jordan has really lifted me. The 'Word
for Today' says, 'Are you expectant of the miraculous intervention
of God?' And I am!

I believe that within the next month we will see God's
provision for CAP and the house will be saved. God will provide
enough for William (Spencer) to join me and we will be able to
move forward and really get CAP going. I see £50,000 to £60,000
being released and then everybody will know the support God
has shown us throughout the last year.

It's wonderful how God can lift your eyes from what you see
to what you know. He can lift your spirit so much. As Philippians
4 says,

'And the peace of God which transcends all understanding
will guard your hearts and your minds in Christ Jesus.'
(Philippians 4:7)

I pray that the next time I write, it will be to record God's
abundant blessing on the ministry and our financial situation.

June 6, 1997

A very tough week. The pressure continues to build but the Lord
continues to provide on a daily basis. On Sunday we were given
£50 by a former client, Jan. That money allowed us to go out with
the girls on Monday. Today we got another £100 which will pay
for the bridesmaid dress and our weekend. We also realised that
we had £24 in savings stamps for Morrisons the supermarket so
we will be able to buy enough food for the next few days. Praise
God for his provision. I continue to fundraise and have 'cast my
bread upon the water.' I have sent over 70 requests for funding.
All I can now do is pray and wait for God to move.

Lizzie and myself have had a good week reading Joshua
and looking at God's promises and today I now know why. We
received the letter from the building society asking us to pay
£3,693.35 arrears on our mortgage. I am struck by how ridiculous

our situation looks. Here I am praising God for the £24 we have got to buy our food, while our mortgage and our house security look so unsure. Yet it is these times when the word becomes life. I'm not desperate about losing the house. I don't think we will and that's nothing to do with what I can see. Far from it! Anybody else would say we have lost the house and we will become homeless. Yet I know deep down in my heart that we have been faithful and that the Lord has commanded a blessing upon us. All I have to do is be strong and courageous and wait for it to come. What will the next few weeks bring? Trials or provision? Yet I expect a miraculous intervention by God into our circumstances, and that we will go away on holiday on July 19 knowing that we are secure in our ministry and that the house is safe.

We have been invited to go on holiday to Wales with some good friends. All we need is a caravan or tent, some money and some time off. I sense that God has got it all in hand. All we have to do is have faith that God would want us to be restored, refreshed and enjoy a holiday. He will do the rest.

The girls have been drawing pictures of caravans and tents and they are praying that God will give us a mobile home or something similar for our family holiday. I'm so touched by their child-like faith and total trust that we will be all right. We never tell them about the true situation but we speak a little about possibly moving to somewhere smaller. They just seem to take it all in their stride.

June 7, 1997

Today we actually crossed a new border of our faith. We have got through the week but if we go out tonight as planned with friends, we have only £19 for food. Should I tell someone? Should I borrow from someone? Difficult decisions! I have decided not to tell anyone and Lizzie will use the money to get us through the weekend. I pray that something will come up on Monday, as we need £90 for our council tax and water rates as well as some more food money.

Praise God for the faith he gives us! I don't feel too bad, I just know that God is faithful in all he promises and his word says in Psalm 37, 'Never have I seen the children of the righteous begging bread.' Amen.

I am so confident that God is faithful that I can now go out and play my part in our outreach today and tomorrow, and I pray that more will come to know the Jesus whom I love and serve.

July 12, 1997

What a four weeks we have just had. Such highs and such lows. Firstly, the provision of a holiday for Lizzie, the girls and myself. We had no money, no caravan, tent, trailer or tow bar however we knew it was right despite our dire financial situation. The girls started to pray and we just knew God would make it happen. Well, over the last four weeks Avril and Chris Gray have not only offered us their wonderful caravan for two weeks, but they will even tow it down to Wales and back! What generosity!

Avril was the first to sow into CAP with a gift of £10 and they were the couple who said we could live in their back garden in their caravan if we had nowhere to live!

July 12, 1997 continued

We then needed money to cover the site costs, petrol and spending money etc. Some friends gave us £500 and said they would pay for our site fees. Words almost fail me when we see God meet our needs in such a dynamic way.

Our house and mortgage situation continue to be very difficult. We are now nearly £4000 in arrears and we have until the end of August – just 50 days – to give the building society some certainty we can pay the mortgage. The enormity of the problem in some ways takes away the worry as there is absolutely nothing we can do but keep working in the ministry.

We have had good support from ten trusts over the last month and financially the charity is in better shape than before, but we still need £2,500 before the end of August to keep going.

I am getting better overall with rejection (everything's relative I suppose!), and the more I work with the people who come to me the more I know this is God's work and the responsibility for funding it is his. I don't have to worry about the overall future of the ministry. My one job is to be faithful in the small things and seek his will for the direction of the work.

Lizzie and I have been having some difficulties over the last month. I have been quite sharp with her. I sense that the pressure of a front line ministry has an impact on your closest relationships. God has to put me back on the right path!

After a six-year battle I finally won an amazing final victory over the one remaining credit card collection company that had given me such a hard time. When I started the legal action over their refusal to accept my offer, they said my action was wrong. However, they would now accept my offer. I have to pay just £10 a month for the next five years on a total debt of £3,000. With this final acceptance, I now only have to pay £7,000 on the £24,000 I owe. I remember in 1992 when everything collapsed I owed £78,000. To think that in five years I will have cleared everything is a huge relief. What a gracious and providing God![2]

---

2   Over the next five years we managed to make every agreed repayment to my creditors and in May 2002 we paid our last repayment! The feeling of being debt free, apart from mortgage and hire purchase on my car, is one I am determined thousands of people will experience over the coming years as they work with CAP.

CHAPTER SIX

CAP'S FIRST EMPLOYEES

AUGUST 1997 TO MAY 1998

Just over a year into our work our perseverance was beginning to pay off. William Spencer handed in his notice and came to work for CAP as our first real employee.

When William joined, we started to press forward, even though we didn't have the funding. Every single person who has ever worked for us have all joined knowing we didn't have the funding to pay our existing team. However, they have all stepped out in faith and that faith has been vindicated. God has honoured every contract of employment we have ever given out.

August 14, 1997

Today, just over a week since William gave his job up in faith to join me full time, £5,000 came from Trust for the Homeless!

I got to know Roger Carson, who headed the trust, quite well and I still don't think he understands just how much his faith in me meant. This was the first trust to really believe in what we were doing. There will never be another morning quite like the morning when I opened that letter. It broke something. Praise God for men and women of God who have a heart to give.

August 22, 1997

The Tudor Trust have agreed to give us a grant of £8,000! I got the phone call from William and although I had been through so much and knew that God would meet my needs, I could not believe that we were going to be paid for the next few months and that CAP would for the first time, have some financial base.

Just before we went away on holiday, we were given a word from a friend called Sue, who said she had seen a vision of a pillar of smoke over our house and it wasn't moving. She believed that God wanted us to stay in our house. I felt certain that God had granted us the house and although the situation was still very serious. I took the 'For Sale' sign down and managed to pay the full monthly mortgage payment for the first time in over a year. We went on holiday in faith that God would be working on the whole situation while we were away.

September 10, 1997

Things just get better! More finances have come in and we have seen God provide us with some computer equipment through the Lloyds TSB Foundation. Not just any old rubbish either – the very best and latest system, which should be installed over the next couple of weeks.

We have been spending some time looking at Nehemiah, and in particular how he defended the wall when it was half built. We feel God is saying that for the next few weeks we have to defend what He has done so far. We have decided to set things up for the future, establish the office, and develop a new brochure, which would all help with our work. What a feeling to know that you have time to get things right, that you are not chasing money all the time and trying to get the ministry growing in your own strength!

September 16, 1997

While at the Kings Park conference I received the following prophecy:

> *'You have a deposit but you have much more to come into*
> *– bigger than even you can see now. Just keep walking into*
> *it, it's coming towards you. There is more to come!'*

And we have certainly seen some amazing provision in the last few weeks. Trust for the Homeless gave another £5,000! Roger Carson, who headed the trust, said he was so touched by my thank you that he felt God tell him to send me another £5,000!

This man and his wonderful trust have doubled what we received in the first year in just two months! It is such an amazing gesture led by the Holy Spirit. Praise God! Even so, it needed men and women of God to have faith that they had heard right, and generous hearts to actually send the money.[3]

September 16, 1997 continued

The Tudor Trust money came in and we found ourselves with just over £13,000 in the bank. We needed two cars to visit clients and we decided that as Tearfund was expected to give us £10,000, we would wait until it was confirmed on 18 September before buying them.

However, the decision was delayed due to too many proposals on the meeting day, and we would not find out until 1 October. The choice was simple, wait or buy the cars we needed now. We really needed them now, we had only one car which was unreliable, and we were travelling more and more. However, the cost of the cars was two-and-a-half months salary and running costs. Praise God we chose the option of faith. We

---

3   Under God's guidance this trust distributed its funds and closed in the late nineties. Roger remains a great supporter of the charity and a personal friend.

bought two cars and left ourselves with only £2,600 at the end of
September – less than one month's money.

You will not be surprised that Tearfund did agree to our grant. It came
in during October and we continued to move forward in our work.[4]
We also received notification from the Sir Halley Stewart Trust that
they would fund us with £3,000 per quarter starting in January.[5]

This whole area of getting good equipment and hiring staff
irrespective of whether you have the money is one thing that has
marked us out over the years. We get the best computer systems we
can. We have never to this date, made any purchase decision based
on whether we have the money. If we need it, we get it. We have the
faith that God will meet our needs. The testimony to God's provision
is that we have always been able to pay every invoice and bill, even if a
few days late on some occasions. We know the way God has led us has
brought some criticism, but I can only remain true and faithful to how
I feel he has called us to operate.

Time and time again, God has helped us step out in faith. Over the
years our trustees have again and again backed us with these decisions
and not restricted what we need due to perceived lack of finance. This
has meant that in practice we may have looked foolish and unwise but,
believe me, if there had been another way, we would have done it. Faith
to me is when you step out into the unknown. It is being certain of a
future hoped for but not yet seen.

   "Faith is the conviction of things not seen"

                                        (Hebrews 11:1 RSV).

---

4   Tearfund supported us until 2002. We have been so grateful to them for their
involvement with us, and we very much look up to them as a standard to reach for, in
how they operate as a Christian organisation..
5   The Sir Halley Stewart Trust was to become one of the most encouraging we have
ever had. They supported us for six years, until to 2003.

It's easy to believe in things we can see, but not so easy to believe in the things we cannot see. Yet this is exactly where faith operates. We do not need faith to operate in the realm of things we can see; it is sight, not faith that operates there.

Faith operates in the realm of things the physical eye cannot see, and is able, as the writer to the Hebrews puts it, to 'see the invisible.' This is not a contradiction, but a paradox. A paradox is something that may seem contrary to reason, but nevertheless is true.

Faith is a paradox. Faith sees the invisible, knows the unknowable, hears the inaudible and touches the intangible. It fights in chains and rests in conflict. Contradictory? No – paradoxical and therefore true.

> 'Now faith is being sure of what we hope for and certain of what we do not see.'"

> 'And without faith it is impossible to please God, because anyone who comes to him must believe that he exists and that he rewards those who earnestly seek him.'
>
> *(Hebrews 11:1, 6)*

Over the next three months things got going and we came into a new sense of God's provision. Even after such a traumatic first year we did not hold back. We never said, 'let's stop and stay where we are.' We just pressed on with looking for another full-time member of staff and growing the work. The next member of staff was Ruth Graves. Ruth worked at Lloyds TSB near our house and back in June 1996 when I paid the first £10 into the bank, she was the cashier that took the money. She asked about CAP, became a 'Life Changer' and always asked me about the work whenever I paid money in. She came to see what we did and then decided to give up her very secure job to join us. She left without any redundancy and was such a blessing to us.

November 22, 1997

Today we received an acceptance letter from Ruth Graves in answer to our job offer. Again what faith God has given us! Here we are with only two months money, no sign of any great outpouring of finance, and we have agreed to offer a job to Ruth. What is even more spectacular is that she knows that we have no funding at present but is prepared to give up her job at the bank where she has worked for 11 years to work for us.

Here is an extract from her letter.

'The first thing is that God has specifically called me to work alongside you in your ministry. God has prepared me to join CAP. As far as finances go, I do understand the 'faith' element that the ministry operates in. In fact, I wouldn't want it any other way. I look forward to seeing God provide for our needs. I know that God is true to his word Phil 4:19, 'and my God will meet all your needs in his glorious riches in Christ Jesus.' I will have no hesitation in handing in my notice on January 1, even if my redundancy does not come through.'

She ended her letter with two bible passages.

'Now to him who is able to do immeasurably more than all we ask, or imagine, according to his power that is at work within us, to him be glory.'

(Ephesians 3:20–21)

'Wait for the Lord; be strong and take heart and wait for the Lord.'

(Psalm 27:14)

This has to be one of the most amazing job acceptance letters ever. I can just feel her total faith that God was in her decision and that it was her destiny to join CAP. We need to remember that at this time it was just a very small ministry with two blokes working from a bedroom office in a house that looked like it might be repossessed. Outstanding faith or what!

November 27, 1997

Over the last few days, Caroline Bateman has come to see us and it can only be God who has brought her. Together with her husband she has supported us from the beginning and didn't really know us. She feels that God is calling her into our ministry, and she is obviously talented and well able to be a great blessing to our ministry.

The only problem is that hiring someone will take our monthly expenses up to £7,000 and we only have enough to pay William and myself until the end of January at the most.

On top of all that, we have heard that our application for funding from Bradford Council has been turned down for something about our constitution. They just didn't want to fund us.

On the other hand Franco Fotti, who is a friend of ours from Cleveland, Ohio, was with us on Tuesday night and gave us the following prophecy:

'God starts at the end, he knows the end from the beginning. Your ministry will be talked about in every paper in the land. You will come before kings and rulers.

You will pour out blessings and abundance, not because of you but because of God and for his glory in the nation. Be a vessel. Enlarge your tent – greater than you imagine. Hold steady at times of testing. God will finish what he has established.

He will not lead you where he does not feed you. He will not guide you where he will not provide. Continue to walk in obedience.'

What a word! As we look to the next couple of months and 1998, I sense the word in Ecclesiastes,

"Whoever watches the wind will not plant; whoever looks at the clouds will not reap."

(Ecclesiastes 11:4)

If I looked to the circumstances, I would just sit tight and wait until some money comes in and then move. If I had waited for the circumstances to change and become favourable I would never have started CAP. If I had felt that circumstances reflected what God thought of our ministry and myself, I would have packed it in many times. Praise God for his word and his encouragement through brothers and sisters. I am taking tomorrow off to spend the day away from work. I have lots and lots to do but it can all wait, and I sense it is a time of reflection at the end of a truly amazing year. The next four weeks are crucial in the run up to Christmas, very busy and with lots of decisions to make. Our prayer letter went out today along with 60 videos of clients saying thank you to everybody who has supported our ministry. Malcolm West has done a fantastic job making our video, giving his time and talent free of charge. I pray people will respond to our work but I am beginning to see that it is not by my might or in my power but by his Spirit. I pray people will be moved to support us in prayer and in practical finance, and I just know that God will provide the £100,000 we will need next year. I know this because I know we are in his will, doing his work. He 'knows the end from the beginning,' and is not altered from his goal by man and his reactions to events. Praise God!

December 27, 1997

Looking back, I am struck by just how far we've come with God's help. Last year at this time I was on my own and had just begun CAP. Over the year we have proved beyond any doubt that with God's help, we can make a real difference in people's lives. Letter after letter from people tell me that we are changing their lives. We know that our work is being used by God to set the captives free and people are getting saved.

We have also learned that not everyone takes up our offer of help. We have been disappointed and let down by our clients along the way. The secret must be to use the very precious and limited resources at our disposal to best effect. We have no alternative but to move on if clients we help are not responding.

Caroline Bateman, William Spencer, myself, Ruth Barber (née Graves)
(Photograph reproduced by kind permission of the Telegraph and Argus, Bradford)

You can lead a horse to water but you can't make it drink. Because we are looking for sustainable poverty relief, we have to empower clients to trust us and change how they live. If they refuse to work with us there is nothing we can do. We need to concentrate on the people we can help and who will work with us. We need to have the confidence in God's ability to bring people back to us if they don't respond first time around. Until then, we have to let them go.

What does 1998 hold for us all? It is the most exciting, challenging and frightening thing I have ever faced. There will be four of us by February with a monthly budget of approximately £8,000. We are £78,000 short of our needs for the whole year and we need £4,000 in January alone. The new staff will need to be trained and the whole dynamics of the ministry will change. Expansion is inevitable and my responsibilities will continue to increase and expand.

We still have great difficulties with our financial situation of a large mortgage and basically insufficient money to meet our needs every month from my salary. But God is so good, we never want for anything. At the moment we have just £50 to last us four weeks, but my faith continues to increase in line with our needs. What will happen with our house and mortgage? Who knows! All I know is that God will do whatever needs to be done to provide us with somewhere to live and give us the ability to meet our commitments, pay our bills and be blessed with abundant provision. That's the heart of my God. He's not stingy. He does not withhold without reason and that can only be for our good in the long term. What a joy it is just to know that you are in God's hands and he takes away the responsibility and pressure. Praise God for that indescribable gift of peace.

February 6, 1998

Caroline Bateman joined us in January as a part-time help with admin and fundraising. With Ruth now with us, the sense of elation at seeing four of us working for CAP is almost impossible to describe. What a resource from God to us for his work in the city. What a wonderful weekend it has been. I was paid £150 from CAP. This meant we could afford to go away and buy Lizzie some boots that she needed. Then over the weekend we received £125 as a gift, and the promise of £250 in a couple of weeks. Then yesterday, another gift of £100 came from a brother down in Aldershot. The result of all this is that we have survived another two weeks, have enough for food for the next week and yet again, God has broken through with his provision.

As far as the charity is concerned, we still need £1,000 this month and £6,000 next month but I just know it will come in. Although I wish we had the money on hand, it's obviously not God's way at the moment. However, I sense that soon, very soon, we are going to be blessed.

The following diary section describes one of the many times we saw God dramatically intervene in a case with CAP. There is always a future hope, always a way forward and with God on our side we need not be fearful of any solicitors, judges or bailiffs. The couple concerned encapsulate the whole work we undertake. It was cases like this, week in week out, that were and remain today our great motivation. I pray you get a sense of what we do and how we work with families to release them from indescribable difficulties.

February 15, 1998

Yesterday (Saturday), I got a phone call from the next-door neighbour of an elderly couple who were in a desperate situation. I went round straight away. Something told me this was a vital one and it required me now. When I got there they were in a desperate state, about to be evicted at 10.30am on Monday! The husband had been told he needed to go into a local psychiatric hospital and he said he would go on Monday if he lost the house.

His wife was suffering from shock. She had been confused and had hidden from him their true financial situation. It was only when the bailiffs called at her house on the Friday and told her to get all the furniture out that she realised what things had come to. The bailiff was reasonable as many are, and could see she hadn't even packed. He actually drove her to court to have the repossession notice suspended until 10.30am Monday, and told the locksmith to go away. Apparently the locksmith was not very happy. I spent about an hour trying to calm the couple down and get enough information to mount a challenge to the repossession order at court on Monday at 10.15am. I felt a tremendous sense of love and compassion for this couple.

If ever I needed confirmation that I was in the right place and in God's will, it was being with this couple. They had nothing and nobody else to help them, they were in shock and unable to comprehend what was happening. They had nowhere to go or to live and were decent elderly people who had fallen on hard times and did not know what to do. I need to appear with them in court on Monday and try to get the repossession suspended. Then I can try and resolve the difficulties which I know, given a couple of months, I can do.

One of the scriptures which comes to mind is in Proverbs. It says,

> *'Do not exploit the poor because they are poor and do not crush the needy in court, for the Lord will take up their case and will plunder those who plunder them.'*
>
> *(Proverbs 22:22-23)*

Praise God that he has taken up their case and he will be with me in court on Monday. He is much bigger than the judge and the landlord's solicitors. I just need to rest in his word and have faith that he will come to the rescue of this couple. This situation is exactly what our ministry is based upon,

> *'Speak up for those who cannot speak for themselves, for the rights of all who are destitute. Speak up and judge fairly; defend the rights of the poor and needy.'*
>
> *(Proverbs 31:8-9)*

> *'You hear, O Lord, the desire of the afflicted; you encourage them, and you listen to their cry, defending the fatherless and the oppressed, in order that man, who is of the earth, may terrify no more.'*
>
> *(Psalm 10:17-18)*

I know that God will be true to his word, and I pray that we win the court case on Monday and keep this lovely couple in their home where they have been for the last thirteen years.

February 16, 1998

What a day! I appeared at court at 10.15am and God miraculously intervened. After two minutes of the landlord's solicitor ranting on and on about how hopeless my client had been, the county court judge told her to, 'Be quiet!' It gave me chance to explain the case and ask for leniency. The judge gave me a 30-day suspension order, and I ran across the courthouse to get to the bailiff's office before they set off at 10.30. I arrived at 10.29, just in time to hand the bailiffs the suspension order.

God is good and what a witness and motivation to everyone associated with CAP! Without our being there and available to help, this couple would have been dumped out on the street with nothing and nowhere to live.

Just to update you with this couple, they became model clients. They paid all their debts off including £1,500 rent arrears, cleared all their other credit and started saving. They moved into sheltered accommodation and were still working with us when they both prayed a prayer of salvation in May 2002. Shortly after this the lady died. Her husband has since also gone to be with the Lord. I can't wait to meet them again. CAP has an eternal aspect just as important as the lives saved here and now.

Over the years we have appeared in court hundreds of times to get repossession orders suspended. Time and time again, providing there is a good enough chance of things being worked out, we have had amazing judgements given to us by sympathetic judges. Literally hundreds of families have followed in the footsteps of this first case and almost every week we hear testimonies of similar supernatural events that save people's homes and keep families together.

February 25, 1998

I had to use the £14 I had put on one side for my daughter's birthday present. However, we got through and God did provide for our food, not exactly as I would have expected. We often want to have enough money for the next few days, the next week or the next month or year, but in the wilderness God provided daily.

Over the last couple of days God has poured out his provision. Three people gave us £50 and when I paid all the bills out, I didn't have to pay the Council Tax for two months, which meant I had over £100 left out of my wage. This is amazing and although it doesn't sound a lot, it's more than the £3.77 I had left last month.

All the staff got paid their wages and again God provided just when we needed it. We were several hundred pounds off paying everyone but we stepped out in faith and wrote the cheques, splitting one salary into two to give God a couple more days. We needn't have bothered, three gifts of £400, which normally take up to four weeks to clear through the banking system, cleared at 10.30am, 14 days earlier than normal. Guess what, our shortfall was just under £400. God is so good and provides in so many ways.

March 17, 1998

I have been so insecure and emotional during the weekend. I got very irritable with Lizzie and went into self-pity mode. We were also very tight for food-shopping money. However, the Lord brought me through and I know that many are praying for us and we will get through, but it's tough.

It's times like this when we have nothing and I can't provide for my family's basic needs that I feel a little let down. God knows my heart and it won't always be like this. He will reward us for our trials and sufferings as the word says:

'Consider it pure joy, my brothers, whenever you face trials of many kinds, because you know that the testing of your faith develops perseverance. Perseverance must finish its work so that you may be mature and complete, not lacking anything.'

(James 1:2-4)

March 23, 1998

A great weekend, even though our personal circumstances were dire. Lizzie had an uncomfortable supermarket experience and had to put food back at the check out. We actually had less than

£1 between us but the great sense of God was wonderful. By his Holy Spirit we were able to praise God in a wonderful way and had tremendous praise and worship over the weekend. We just knew that God would turn up something for us. Then first thing this morning, I came down to an envelope which someone had put through our letterbox. In it was £250 pounds with no indication of who had given it. What an awesome God we have! I could pay what I owed, we gave our tithe and another gift, and we still had enough for next week's food.

I pray the person who put this money through our letterbox will read this and know just how they provided for us. Also, for anyone who has ever given any financial support to anyone without them knowing who gave it, I pray you are encouraged to carry on. To anyone who has never done such a thing, 'Now is the time' says the Lord!

> *'But when you give to the needy, do not let your left hand know what your right hand is doing, so that your giving may be in secret. Then your Father, who sees what is done in secret, will reward you.'*
>
> *(Matthew 6:3-4)*

March 23, 1998 continued

God is so good and faithful. I still don't understand why he waited until this morning. Perhaps he just wanted to see if our praise and worship was based on our circumstances and feelings or on our unconditional love for God. What an honour that through his Holy Spirit we may have begun to learn how to praise him in spirit and truth rather than because life is easy for us on that day.

March 25, 1998

Well, wages day has come and we are still several thousand pounds short. But we have got £1,500 and we know that £5,500 will come in over the next week. Therefore we have all had to sit down and work out what we all need to pay our various standing orders for the next week. We are going to divide what we have according to each person's needs. What a wonderful example of God's people working together. Ruth and Caroline say they can get by for another week which means that both William and I can just clear our standing orders for mortgage and other essential payments. Whoever said being a Christian was boring? It's the most challenging and exhilarating thing I could ever imagine.

This was just one example of the many times staff have favoured each other when wages are due. Still to this day, we share out the wages we have. However, the foundations laid in the early days by the four of us have been very strong, and it remains a testimony to God's people preferring each other, putting the needs of others before their own.

March 25, 1998 continued

We are holding our monthly staff meeting and reviews today, and all our talk will be on the future expansion and ongoing work of our ministry. Can you imagine in the outside world in a normal business a boss sitting down with staff and telling them to pray for their wages? Then asking them to decide who should get what little money you have got, and then start talking about expanding the business and taking on more staff. Are we mad? It is only the grace of God working in our lives that could give us the fruit that we have seen over the last few weeks. What a gift to be content and have a spirit of praise and worship that is unaffected by the circumstances that surround us!

10.30am

After we checked the bank account we were still short. Some money that was expected did not come in. Then the post arrived. Now we have two cheques for £500, both from totally unexpected sources. This means that we can all cover our needs this weekend for standing orders for our mortgages etc. Then when the £5,500 comes in next week we can all be paid and our outstanding bills will be cleared. Praise God for his faithfulness and for his provision, I get a sense that he is not finished yet and that we might be overwhelmed before the end of the week.

May 6, 1998

What a weekend we had! Went to the most wonderful conference at church and it was wonderful to see God's presence and all that went on. Over the weekend we got a letter from the Rank Benevolent Memorial Trust saying they would give us £23,500 over the next three years: £10,000 now and the rest spread over the next two years. God is so good and this gives us some breathing space over the next few weeks. It means that our accounts will be in wonderful shape when we finish our financial year-end at the end of this month.

May 31, 1998

We have just finished our second year, and what a year it was. Our income has grown almost eight-fold from £10,413 in the first year to an amazing £84,796. With more than 160 people helped, more and more people becoming Christians, and three full time and one part time staff members. It's almost impossible to imagine that this time last year I was still on my own, with William just volunteering one day a week. It has been a miracle to see how God has touched our lives and blessed the work of CAP.

We had established the basic debt counselling systems and proved I could train other people to do the debt counselling, and more and more people were becoming Christians! What an amazing second year. I believe that it was the year the foundations were laid for the way CAP changes lives.

CHAPTER SEVEN

GOD SPEAKS: 'DON'T HOLD BACK'

JUNE 1998 TO MAY 1999

All the time the work was expanding, with more families being helped and many getting saved and being added to the church. We were more settled than we had been for two years. Did we pause and catch our breath? I don't think so.

I had always known that the misery of debt we were seeing was not particular to Bradford. I knew that if we were to really begin to make an impact on such a huge nationwide problem we had to find a way to expand the operation without losing the ingredients that made us distinctively church based and evangelistic.

I began to look at the make-up of CAP and what had made us so successful in Bradford. There were four vital things. Firstly we had one church, Christian Life Church, and a leader, Paul Hubbard, who really believed in our work and was able to transmit that enthusiasm to his congregation. Secondly, we needed a person who was willing to join CAP and be trained as a debt counsellor. This person would be the one who would pioneer the work in the church and the town. Thirdly, we needed faith that God would provide. This had to be shared by both the church and CAP. Finally we needed a training and support system based in Bradford to support and keep up the momentum at remote centres.

It's very interesting that in the past I had been involved in expanding consumer finance companies by opening centres in new towns. I now see how this experience of creating 'franchised' workable systems to duplicate and grow any successful business was crucial in helping to launch CAP into the next and most demanding phase.

We had a great relationship with Kings Church, Aldershot, and Derek Brown, the pastor, had invited me to share the vision. I had already helped a couple in the congregation who were struggling with debt issues.

So during the summer we went full steam ahead preparing for the opening of our very first CAP centre in Aldershot. We were beginning to develop the strategy of opening centres. It was a ridiculous thing to do bearing in mind our ongoing needs. Looking back I am stunned by the 'let's just do it' mentality and faith we had. It remains today as another expression of the faith that has been the backbone of CAP.

August 1, 1998

What a last two months that's been, so much has happened at such a pace.

There was the first CAP newspaper which we did over the last eight weeks. It was an incredible venture inspired by God, which took weeks and weeks to complete. We had 26 articles to write, and we also had to learn how to write articles!

Lizzie has just lost her mum and although in some ways it was blessing for her to have no more pain, it has been a very difficult time for Lizzie and her family. She carries so much so well and I don't really appreciate her as I know I should.

We have also moved forward with the vision of a national network of centres with the opening of our first remote centre in Aldershot. God has brought Peter and Avril Wood to head this up. Again this has been led by God and, although there have been some teething problems, we are going ahead again in faith that it's right in God and he will provide for us.

September 19, 1998

Aldershot is now open and although it has been tough, I sense God saying to me, 'Now you know how I feel when you don't live up to my expectations but I still use you and love you despite your actions.' I know that over the next thirty years I will have to deal with many churches and people who disappoint me and who I will disappoint. However, by God's grace we will complete the calling and CAP will play its part in changing a nation through hundreds of imperfect churches and thousands of imperfect people just like me.

Liverpool, Huddersfield, Worcester and South West Nottingham are also beginning to open up. It's so exciting to see God's plans and purposes coming together. I could never have foreseen what joy I feel to play my part in his Great Commission. Let's see how God works out the next month. It's going to be another testimony of his faithfulness and provision.

No money as yet, things just seem to get tighter and tighter. We have to use money that is set aside for other things to pay for food shopping and I have even had to consider using the Visa card that came in today. Maybe God is telling me that I have to have the faith to use my Visa card in the same way that I know he will provide for me to pay it off. We still need £6,000 to be able to pay the wages next week and I have absolutely no idea where the money is to come from.

This week I got the following word,

> *'Enlarge the place of your tent, stretch your tent curtains wide, do not hold back; lengthen your cords, strengthen your stakes. For you will spread out to the right and to the left; your descendants will dispossess nations and settle*

in their desolate cities. Do not be afraid; you will not suffer shame. Do not fear disgrace; you will not be humiliated.'
(Isaiah 54:2–4)

I feel this speaks directly to me about strengthening my foundations, just opening up and spreading out. It also says that we will not suffer shame and that we will not be humiliated. I know that God will not let us down as we step out in faith to pay people properly and expand our work. My prayer is 'quickly Lord.'

This was the first time I was drawn to those verses in Isaiah. It was just one of those times when reading his word that you feel in your spirit that God himself wrote those words for you. Over the years it has become one of our most important scriptures and has been a real encouragement to press ahead. It's framed in my office and virtually every day I read it and meditate on God's promises in these few short verses.

Each time we have opened centres we have not had the money to pay even the first month's wages. It's as if we are tested at each point of expansion. Each time we have said, 'Nevertheless, let's press forward.' I particularly like verse four, which says, 'Do not be afraid; you will not suffer shame. Do not fear disgrace; you will not be humiliated.'

I realise now this shame and humiliation is in the Lord's eyes, not in the hearts or words of men and women. Many times I have suffered shame before man and been humiliated by our lack. However, I know that the Lord has never been ashamed or humiliated by what we do and I believe there is great honour when you suffer at the hands of men for a God-inspired vision.

October 5, 1998

Well, God was true to his word and we did get paid. Eventually a series of miracles happened. Firstly, a client called, who had sold his house to clear his debts and make a fresh start, and to our astonishment said he wanted to sow £2,000 into the ministry. Secondly, one of the couples who came to see us about setting up a centre in Nottingham sent £1,000 from their church's trust fund.

Several Trusts sent a few hundred pounds. We have just paid all our bills and still have about £1,500 for this month only £6,000 to go. It's incredible to look back and see how faithful God is.

We have just had a Trustees' meeting where our plans to open ten new centres were approved. This means that by the middle of next year, May 1999, we will have ten centres reaching out into their communities.

On a less positive note we were forced to use a small overdraft from the bank to pay everybody we owed money to, which now means we need about £2,000 to get everything paid off. Only God knows how this will all work out.

This was a crucial point for CAP. Did we step out and hire the staff or did we hold back? I still can't quite believe we actually sent out the job offers and contracts. There is always a point where there is no going back; where you become totally reliant on God, when you go beyond your own and anyone else's understanding or rational thoughts. This was that point of no return, from this point the bridges were well and truly burnt.

October 21, 1998

As the weeks have progressed the financial situation has become more desperate. Here I am, wanting to take on three new staff when I am about £5,000 short of paying the wages of the ones I already have. By Friday nothing had come in and I was faced with the decision about sending out the job offers to the new staff. I felt deep down that it was right to go for it. I felt God saying, 'If it's right, act as if you have the money and send out the job offers.' I sent them out and waited to see where the money to pay us all would come from. Saturday's post came and went. Nothing, no money. Nevertheless, I just carried on with the weekend and thought very little about our predicament.

October 25, 1998

It is my birthday and unbeknown to me, Lizzie and the staff had pulled out all the hand written mail for me over the week thinking they were birthday cards. As I opened one, out fell a cheque for £6,000 from a man I had spoken to earlier in the week. From his letter it appears that he suffered great financial hardship in the 80s and longed for some practical help like CAP offers. He said he wanted to bless our work with some of the immeasurable blessing God had given him.

The letter came into the office on Thursday morning so when I sent the job offers out the cheque was only a few inches away from me but I didn't know. God just wanted to know whether my decision was based on what I could see in terms of finance and what I knew to be the right thing to do.

Praise God for his faithfulness. I pray the couple who sent this cheque understand the significance of their gift.

November 27, 1998

Just one month since that fantastic miracle of £6,000 on my birthday, here we go again.

We even had to divide up what money we had amongst the staff this week and it is always a very humbling thing to see staff preferring each other in terms of paying salaries. Nothing came in until the last phone call at 5.45pm on Friday from Tear Fund saying they had agreed another grant for £10,000. We would get this within the next ten days. I wonder if they really know just how vital their encouragement is to us on the front line. Anyway this meant that even if we had to borrow, we could all get paid the next week. I somehow got a sense that God hadn't finished yet.

Here again we see Tear Fund's support just in time. I hope
David Evans, who helped with these first few years support,
understands just what it meant to us.

On Sunday a couple from our church gave us £323 and after
William had added in the regular income we could expect over
the next few days we were just £1,000 short. Then on Monday,
at about 11am, a pastor and amazing man of God from a local
church called in unexpectedly. We had added a couple of our
clients to his congregation. He just gave us a cheque for £500
from the church and £500 from himself. I was totally taken aback
by the generosity of this church and this pastor. It was as if an
angel had walked among us. We finished the month with £150
to spare and knowing we would get paid in December. This was
only the second month in two years that we had the wages at the
beginning of the month. Praise God for his provision.

January 18, 1999

Things are really starting to hot up. We are now on the threshold
of a new year and I can't quite imagine what it has in store. By
the end of the month there will be 14 people working for CAP.
Our monthly needs in terms of salaries etc will have risen to
£14,000. A huge amount when you consider that we only have
about £2,000 per month in regular income. We really need about
£6,000 this month to pay the National Insurance and tax bill for
December and January, and then £12,000 in February.

I don't know if its fear, the flesh or God but I really sense that
we need to move up a gear in terms of income. Trust income
seems to be slowing down with fewer repeat donations and no
real new ones to go for. What should I do and why does finance
play such a huge part in my thinking? God knows what we need
and I am certain all the finance will come in but will it always be
hand-to-mouth? We need to be honourable in our finances and
pay people, National Insurance and tax on time. Will God bring

someone who pours some real finance into us soon or will we get the money on the drip each and every month? This is now the 23rd out of 25 months when we have started without enough money to pay the wages for the month.

The insolvency work with clients is really getting going. Yet straight away we are running into problems with finance companies refusing to help us. We have a huge amount of work to do to make the service work. It will take time and effort to drive it forward.

Matt and Josie Barlow are coming to Bradford this weekend and are joining us from 1 February. What a joy it will be when they join us and increase the resources here in Bradford by 40 per cent.

Matt and Josie joining was a key event in the life and history of this ministry. They moved from Cheltenham, gave up two good jobs and made a major commitment to CAP. They continue to be very close both as friends and as work colleagues. Matt is now the UK Chief Executive, running the whole UK operation and the support departments. He has played a huge role in developing the operational work of CAP. He is a great and effective manager with wisdom and discernment.

Josie is our Head of Communications and has lead our funding and communications teams over the years she has been with us. They are an amazing couple who have done so much for CAP.

They are the type of people who will see when I am struggling and have a way of lifting me and supporting me through some very difficult times. They are full of faith and both have the amazing and rare ability to make things happen around them.

Matt and Josie have both made such a difference to how CAP has grown and they have laid down a foundation upon which the Lord will build for many years and generations to come.

Matt's Story

'Since giving myself to Jesus in 1992 (six weeks before John), God has given me two passions. One is to care for the poor and needy and the other is to lead people to know God and have their lives transformed. Two years spent in the Dominican Republic gave me great experience at doing these things, but I was sure that there must be some way of doing the same in the UK.

You can imagine how excited I was when this bloke from Yorkshire came to speak at our church in Cheltenham. So off I set on a mission to open my own CAP centre - little did I know where it would lead me!

Within hours of being with John, after he had barely got to know me and even less of Josie, he was offering us both jobs. We weren't aware that the previous week John and Paul had prayed and asked God for two people. Someone to help run centres and someone to work in fundraising. (Josie had been training in fundraising over the previous year.) We prayed like mad and felt God speak to us in a number of ways. Josie then visited Bradford and within six weeks we had given up our jobs, given notice on our flat and moved to Bradford.

Since that time both Josie and I have had the awesome privilege of being at John and Lizzie's side serving both them and God to see people released from oppression and many come to know Jesus through the work of CAP.

It has been a challenging time in many ways but it has also been a real privilege to see God taking the gifts that he had given us in the first place and using them way beyond anything we thought we would ever achieve.

We have seen the power of encouragement, the power of belief in others, trusting them and letting them just "have a go." We have seen the need to be well organised, practical and strategic while constantly being open to God and allowing him to do things however he wants.

Every testimony that comes in of mothers using their new budget and talking of the "luxury" of having £50 per week for food bowls me over. People talk of the amazing feeling of being able to buy Christmas presents with their own money. Perhaps one of the biggest ones for me is the husbands and wives who are still together as a result of our work.

Above all else, the reason we do what we do is to help people discover Jesus. God has told me we are evangelists who do debt counselling, not debt counsellors who do evangelism. To see the smiles and the tears and the transformed lives makes absolutely every difficulty and every challenge worth it.'

Matt Barlow, UK Chief Executive

By early 1999, Lizzie was seven months pregnant and our house had been converted to four offices with seven to ten people working there every day! We needed a home, somewhere Lizzie could have her first child and we could be separated from the work for our sanity! As you will see, yet again God provided for us just in time.

January 18, 1999 continued

Our house needs are still causing me great concern. A Christian brother has said that he will buy us a house and we can then rent it from him at a reduced amount. He would then let us buy the house from him when we can. There is little hope of us getting a mortgage for about two years. The only problem is that he never seems to phone me with an answer to anything and I am beginning to doubt if he is serious. It must be God who is driving this thing forward. Lizzie is now seven months pregnant; we need somewhere to live soon and we have no resources other than God. I pray that God will move soon and find us a house. We feel a bit under pressure.

I also sense that people are beginning to say that we have grown too big, too soon as a charity and we should draw back. Even the Prayer Team's notes seemed to suggest we might be off track and that I needed to be more holy etc. I know all this but I still feel we are exactly where God wants us to be and within his ability to steer us forward. I have got my great brother in

Paul (Hubbard) who I know would shout if he felt I was going off track. I know that despite what other people may think, we are right to step out in complete faith in God. As the word says it is IMPOSSIBLE to please God without faith. I am certain that he will provide for all our needs and that he has grown CAP – not me – and where he leads, he feeds. I know that God will carry on with his faithful support of our ministry.

February 20, 1999

A good month as far as the charity work goes. We are moving forward on every front. With Matt and Josie starting we have got all departments moving forward. The Bradford Centre continues to do well with its manager, Sue Forrest, pushing the Prayer and Ministry team forward very well. Centre Operations and Insolvency Teams are really starting to get going with Matt working very well alongside Ruth.

Fundraising has also moved forward with the completion of the 16-page, four-year development plan that is just being printed. Josie is now working with me on fundraising and I am confident that by June we will be in good shape.

Our problem remains the same as always, finance. We are now in debt owing two months National Insurance (£5,000), needing £7,000 to pay the wages due in five days as well as another £5,000 in bills etc. Never before have the figures been so big and with nothing on the horizon. What can I say? That's how it is and God is big enough to handle my disappointment that yet again, we are down to a few days and the amounts are getting bigger.

Today I received a very hard letter from a brother who has a trust who could have given us a considerable gift. Not only did he not help us but wrote to me saying he felt we had grown too fast and that we were misguided in our plans and that I should ask God for clarity and go back to him with my amended plans.

I actually wrote back to him and said that I had tried to understand his comments but that I was certain we were doing it God's way and that the work would go on irrespective of what others thought. I am stunned when people doubt whether we are in God's will. People are getting saved each month, the poor are being released from poverty and we are the ones paying the price through uncertainty. Everything we do is for others. We are sold out to reach a nation and it is God who leads the way. I'm only responding to his call and his voice that has always said, 'go forward.' Still we wait to see if we are to get our new home and Lizzie is now seven-and-a-half months pregnant. We are now waiting for the building society to agree to us getting a mortgage then we need to find somewhere and complete and move in, all in a few weeks.

Yet again it all seems surreal, here we are agreeing in faith to go on holiday in August when I don't have any food money after Thursday next week, have no house to move into, and a baby on the way.

We owe two months' tax and National Insurance which is hard to handle. However, I have just read Romans 13. It talks about submission to authorities says,

'Give everyone what you owe him; If you owe taxes, pay taxes, if revenue pay revenue; if respect, then respect; if honour, then honour.'

(Romans 13:7)

I know that God will honour our commitment, meet our wages, needs and give us the ability to pay taxes. 'When' and 'how' are the only unknowns and who am I to second guess God? He can do what he wants but I know that it will ultimately be for our good.

Just to testify to God's provision we have eventually paid every tax and National Insurance due. Praise God!

February 20, 1999 continued

We seem to be in a cycle of great need and last minute provision, I wonder if this will always be the way. Will there ever be a day when we have a little spare? Will it always be last minute? Will every decision be in faith for his financial provision?

Nevertheless, only God knows and it's my duty to simply carry on regardless of circumstance and any doubts that people may share with me. God knows how I feel and what pressure Lizzie and I are under. He must be preparing us for something beyond our imagination because I never imagined that I would be faced with such difficulties, pressures, fears and lack of understanding when I started CAP nearly three years ago.

May 21, 1999

What a wonderful three months we have had.

We did get a house, praise God! Elim church offered us their manse that is a four-bedroom detached house on the other side of Bradford. They only wanted one month's rent and even paid for us to decorate and carpet the house. Just in time. Lizzie was eight months pregnant when we moved into the new and beautiful house. God is so good and I will be eternally grateful in particular to Bob McDonald (Pastor of Elim Church) for his encouragement and help at this time.

The highlight was the birth of our daughter Abigail, born 13 April weighing 6lbs 9oz. What a wonderful month and the baby and Lizzie are doing so well. The birth was very traumatic with Lizzie having to have an emergency section after 15 hours of labour. Praise God for the medical services we have and God's hand of protection on our beloved daughter. It's at times like this when everything is put into perspective; it's when you realise what's really important and just how much you have to praise God for.

May 31, 1999

The whole ministry continues to expand with 25 clients seen last month, almost as many as I saw in the whole first year. The team is growing here in Bradford to meet the challenge of the ever increasing demands of the centre network.

Regular giving continues to grow and should reach approximately £3,500 in May, which is wonderful. Churches continue to give generously and I can see a bright future in terms of finance. It's just now that it feels very difficult.

Our year end was on 31 May and by some miracle we managed to pay all our outstanding bills except our wages for May. This has meant that the accounts show we actually balanced our books over the 12 months with an income of £157,460 and an expenditure of £161,366, a miracle in anyone's books.

Our third year drew to a close and, as always, somehow the money had just come in. We now had seven CAP centres (up from just one a year ago), had helped 329 people and seen our income grow from £84,796 to £157, 460. We had seen many lives changed and many come to know the Lord. We had proved the principle of churches catching the vision and reaching out to the poor.

We had seen great advances in what we did. We were beginning to get to grips with what it means to run remote centres and how to train, motivate and inspire people to follow a clearly defined vision. God had continued to be faithful and we were learning fast. I truly believe that the risks we had taken to start opening centres in the UK would be vindicated and we would see this nation transformed through our work.

What was the next year to hold for us? I somehow knew it would be a rough ride and that our characters would be tested again and again.

CHAPTER EIGHT

HARD TIMES

JUNE 1999 TO MAY 2000

The following chapter describes one of the most difficult periods in CAP's history. During these few months I really had to dig so deep, as it was very challenging and frequently painful. As you will see, the diary entries are very raw and I was often on the verge of real anger towards God, but in hindsight I recognise that he understood how I was feeling and he carried me through the whole process.

July 16, 1999

As always finance, or lack of it, continues to cause me the most difficulties. Today William, who manages the situation with great skill and under great pressure, told me we needed approximately £30,000 to pay all our bills and the wages that are due over the next two weeks. We have only £3,000 in funds so to honour our commitments and bills we need £27,000 in two weeks!

When, O God, will you open up your storehouse and allow me to pay all my bills and wages on time? That is all I ask. Not for £150,000 in the bank (although not having to work as hard and commit as many resources to fundraising and to be released from the grind of every increasing need would be wonderful).

Only God knows. I just wish he would release the pressure and open up his storehouse door a little wider.

Who knows what the next few days and weeks over the summer will bring. The Lottery Fund decision will be made on Tuesday although we will not know for several weeks, that's £44,000 and would take the pressure off overnight.

Let's see how God will take us through the next few weeks.

I just want to explain our stance on applying for Lottery Fund money. I realise this is a controversial issue and people have many different views. Firstly, I want to say that anyone or any organisation, church or charity who decides on a different way to ours that you have my complete support. Our decision was based on some simple things we felt were relevant to us.

We prayed and sought God. All the Trustees and Management were involved in coming to the decision that we should at least apply. We realised that when we looked at the application procedure, a seventy-page business plan and massive questioning of what we did, that God could easily close the door if he did not want us to get the money. We were very careful that we did not in any way hide our objectives, one of which is, 'The advancement of the Christian faith.' Nor did we conceal all the biblical reasons why we do what we do. We therefore applied in the January and asked for £225,000 over three years (this was only 20% of our expected needs).

July 29, 1999

Today, we got the wonderful news that the Lottery has decided to support our application with three year funding that amounts to £225,000. There is such joy in the place and the sense of relief is almost indescribable. You only realise just how much you need something when you actually get it.

There's lots to do before we get a penny and it will take several weeks before we receive any funds and we are still in

great need at present with needs totalling over £20,000 and no
idea where the funds will come from.

August 6, 1999

Today I got a summary of our actual financial needs from William,
before he goes away tonight, and I have never faced such a
situation. We need £28,669.59 for all our bills and to pay the
wages due, which are already two weeks late. We only have just
over £100 in the bank.

We have nothing on the horizon except a general promise
from Empire Stores and Laing Trust. What can we do? It is
just overwhelming and we are all feeling the pressure. This is
a particularly difficult time, right in the middle of summer and
holidays. We have nothing of ourselves left and there is real need
among staff.

In the midst of this, I have just been visited by a man from
a trust fund regarding my complaint that for the second time
we had again not even been considered funding. What a
horrendous time, absolutely no encouragement, no flexibility and
no recognition that our work was good. Just confirmation that we
will not be supported. He even said that if he personally had any
money he would not give us any![6]

The fund has rejected us because our clients are encouraged
to make very small donations back to our work. Also we are
affecting the whole nation by having a branch network that
means we do not affect local communities, apparently. In real
terms we were too small three years ago and now we are too big!

Yesterday, William had spoken to the Tax Office about our
overdue tax and National Insurance payments of just over
£7,500. He was verbally threatened with County Court action and
a visit if we did not pay all our outstanding National Insurance
contributions within a few days. We felt hurt at the aggressive

---

6   This was a difficult event for me to handle. This man made me feel terrible. I wonder
if he knew just how difficult and hurtful he was, I honestly think he had no idea and I
don't know which is worse.

way the Tax Office lady dealt with us. What a threat. God says in his Word we should pay our taxes and he will uphold his own commandment. Fear not.

Now I have just taken a call from the Inland Revenue. They said they might have to visit us to see how we were handling the charity and our obligations to tax and National Insurance. (Another threat!)

I can't believe that we have reached such an appalling state of affairs. We are virtually penniless with no ability to pay bills now due. We have no option but to stand in faith or simply lie down and almost die. That's how I feel. My flesh and body are completely at an end. There's almost a refreshing feeling to be so totally overwhelmed by a situation that you can do absolutely nothing about.

Many thoughts come into your mind at times like this. What did we do wrong? How can God allow us to suffer such shame and humiliation in his name. What an appalling witness we are to the world, how could God allow this?

I have no answers, however one thing I know is that it's not over yet and all I can do is just stand and be strong, trusting that my God will see us through. One verse that I have been meditating on today confirms this.

In Acts it says,

'The apostles left the Sanhedrin, rejoicing because they had been counted worthy of suffering disgrace for the Name' (of Jesus).

(Acts 5:41)

Even now I will stand on Isaiah 54,

'… Do not be afraid; you will not suffer shame. Do not fear disgrace; you will not be humiliated.'

(Isaiah 54:2-4a)

The overwhelming factual evidence that surround me says I am wrong, that I am in disgrace and humiliated. Somehow that does not affect the fact that deep down I know we are not humiliated in God's eyes and that he will get us through simply because he said he would.

As a staff team we prayed and comforted each other. Perhaps God knew that we had to just take it today. We decided that there were only three things we had to do. First Ruth phoned the bank but they refused an overdraft. Second I called Paul [Paul Hubbard my Pastor]. He already knew our situation and to his credit he managed to lend £3,000 of his own money just to pay one of the National Insurance bills. What a man of God!

I finally called a long time supporter of our work. He is a wonderful brother who runs a financial services company and I knew he would not be fazed by our plight. I explained our situation and he said he would try to find someone to help us out. What a brother and man of God!

October 8, 1999

What a two months that was. I really do not know how we managed to get through. The Lottery Fund eventually sent £14,000 towards the end of August and we have just struggled on from there. We reached new lows (or highs depending on how you look at things) when at the end of September none of the staff had been paid for two months. Every hope we had did not materialise. We were turned down by several trusts and had to borrow money on our credit cards, not pay suppliers and juggle the money.

Last week reached a new crisis. We needed £35,000 to clear our bills and wages and had nothing coming in. We had also reached the point of real hardship being experienced by staff and their families. Some were almost begging and borrowing to maintain mortgages, food, bills etc. How could this be allowed to go on? I felt dreadful and sick inside. What had I led people into? They trusted me and the vision yet where was God?

Every part of my flesh was screaming out, 'I can't take any more it's just too painful.' Yet a still small voice said carry on, and an even bigger voice inside my mind said I have no option what else can I do? I've come this far. I'm not stopping now.

I made a momentous decision to ring a close friend and ask if he would lend us £15,000. He agreed in such a gracious and encouraging way and although I knew this was getting serious I just had to do something. Several staff members and Trustees felt very unhappy and to be honest, we all struggled.

At a Trustee meeting yesterday it was very difficult. The Trustees were led into fear and doubt by one person about how we were funded and there were suggestions we should stop expanding and cut back on salaries. I felt so empty. Who apart from Paul, would have said, 'The work goes on whatever the circumstances?' Eventually we agreed to borrow the £15,000 next week to pay some wages and some suppliers but the pressure is never far away. Still £10,000 short of every bill and only two weeks before another £15,000 of wages and bills are due.

This next entry was, and still is, a bit shocking to me as I re-read it. I know that it was all bound up with being challenged and tested by fear and mans' thoughts. I also had on a daily basis client after client whose lives were being changed, people were becoming Christians throughout the country and we had long passed the point of no return. I was also surrounded by staff who believed, with me, that we just had to carry on. What amazing people God had brought around me for such a test as what was about to befall us. The morale of the staff was very high, we all knew what we had joined and stood shoulder to shoulder and not for one minute did anyone say we should stop.

October 8, 1999 continued

Someone said to me, 'What are you prepared to do to keep going?' The suggestion was that borrowing was a bridge too far. People don't understand just how far and to what lengths I am prepared to go and have gone to keep CAP afloat. If only people understood how much people need our help and the eternal

value of our struggle to reach people. They have no one to turn
to. They are in such desperate situations.

Another point of difficulty was when my pay was reviewed
by the Trustees when I left the meeting. What hurt me was that
when I wasn't there they somehow managed to revert back to
asking if they could afford a certain amount. There was no sense
of faith, encouragement or support towards me. I felt that this
was the only time in maybe a year that they needed to step out
in faith for me and they didn't. In the end I resolved that my faith
was in God. It is he who supports and encourages me. He is my
provider, not the Trustees or the finances of the charity.

As it turned out there was one Trustee who had basically argued very
strongly about reducing our expenditure to our expected income. It
was more a case that other Trustees could not stand up to the logical
and rational arguments. It was as if they were spectators to the work
and faith we were showing. Each one in turn realised they needed to
increase their own faith and belief in how we operated. This was a
turning point in the charity. As it happened we were going to need this
increased strength over the next few weeks and months. There was a
challenge coming that they needed to be sharpened up for.

God is wonderful! Only he could use such an event to move the
Trustees to a new level of faith and determination so that still today
the Management Board continue as men and women of God who have
their own faith and belief in what we do and will regularly step out in
faith to support our plans.

October 21, 1999

The loan from my friend has caused a great deal of debate.
Many simply felt it was not right. Others understood that I could
do nothing else. It was as if God wanted to know whether other

people had faith to repay a loan and that God can provide however he wants.

I felt desperate in the middle of all the pressure and had no real answer for anyone. I wondered who would press forward were I not here. I believe that there is only my Pastor Paul and a few very close employees like Matt, Josie, William, Caroline and Ruth who really understand my heart. One person said, 'You would do anything, even borrow money to keep this charity going.' They said it in quite a critical way. If only they knew that I have already suffered and given up so much for this work of God and I would give everything up to keep it going.

As so often it is the word of God that gives me most comfort and encouragement to carry on.

'Here is my servant, whom I uphold, my chosen one in whom I delight; I will put my spirit on him and he will bring justice to the nations.'

(Isaiah 42:1)

'I took you from the ends of the earth, from its farthest corners I called you. I said: "You are my servant; I have chosen you and have not rejected you. So do not fear, for I am with you; do not be dismayed, for I am your God. I will strengthen you and help you; I will uphold you with my righteous right hand."'

(Isaiah 41:9–10)

'The poor and needy search for water, but there is none; their tongues are parched with thirst. But I the Lord will answer them; I, the God of Israel, will not forsake them. I will make rivers flow on barren heights, and springs within the valleys. I will turn the desert into pools of water, and the parched ground into springs.'

(Isaiah 41:17–18)

October 22, 1999

Yesterday I had some doubt about where we were going for the first time in ages. Even after the loan and the other promised

money William showed me a list of bills and wages still to pay.
I just felt low, as if there is no end to it all. I am interviewing
three new staff, opening two new centres and pressing ahead in
virtually all departments as if money was no object. The actual
circumstances are screaming stop! Consolidate! I wanted to
speak to Paul, but he's not well and I just have to listen to what
God says.

Ecclesiastes 11 says it all:

> 'Whoever watches the wind will not plant; whoever looks at
> the clouds will not reap.'
>
> (Ecclesiastes 11:4)

We will not hold back because we have no money. We've never
had any money and it has never stopped us. We will continue to
act as if money was no object and God will deliver us from this
place of famine and hardship. No surrender!

This word has been a regular source of encouragement for us at CAP.
It speaks to me and says it never looks like it is the right time to do
anything. It always looks like it's all over. What we can see will always
put us off doing things. Praise God for his word and the way so many
have stood with me and sown when it looked hopeless. It's part of the
DNA God has given us and this decision was a defining point in the
history of CAP.

October 31, 1999

In the midst of all that is going on it's still the families and the
amazing changes we see that drive me forward. The work itself
is absolutely wonderful. People are getting saved almost every
week. We are growing in ability, confidence and drive to move
forward despite our financial worries and difficulties. The word
says it is impossible to please God without faith. Well in that case
he should be very pleased with us.

Giving up or turning back is not an option for us, hundreds of
families rely on us for their future hope. In a nutshell we are in

a place of total reliance on God with no alternative other than to hang on in there. Our wonderful clients need us. We can't stop and abandon them. However hard it is for us - it is even harder for them.

November 8, 1999

A very difficult time at present, a series of pressure points have left me in a terrible state. God is obviously moving through our work. Over the last two weeks we have seen a massive increase in people coming to know Jesus at our church. On Sunday at least two people gave their lives to Jesus and another four were at church. Deep down I know we are on the right track. Last month 45 families were helped by CAP. That's an amazing increase and we are starting to press forward. Only one centre is struggling in terms of clients and we know that God will sort that out, especially as such wonderful people are involved.

I am starting to exhibit classic signs of stress. It is strange. Many times I have trained and helped people to spot stress and here I am exhibiting all the signs. I have lost my appetite and am easily angered. I just feel numb.

The pressure on Lizzie is also growing. She is wonderful and understanding and she does try to understand how I am so easily upset and have such mood swings. I was almost unable to go to work today. It's just too much to bear on my own. I went and opened up to Matt, Josie and Paul and told them that I was in a desperate place and they were totally with me and just held me up in prayer.

When will the pressure be released, what is God trying to hone in me that is still lacking and holding me back? I feel lost. My faith has wobbled over the last few days. I even thought that I could not face another member of staff not getting paid.

I have repented of my sin of lack of faith however the evidence against God intervening is growing. The thought of having to carry on and on with such a lack of finance leaves me wondering if I have got enough within me to sustain another few years.

Psalm 102 speaks of a man who is destitute.

'He will respond to the prayer of the destitute; he will not despise their plea.'

'For it is time to show favour to her; the appointed time has come.'

(Psalm 102:17, 13b)

Oh, if this was the appointed time for God to reveal his abundance of provision to CAP.

November 12, 1999

Another terrible day. I spoke to a Trustee on the phone and I am absolutely devastated with the fact that it looks as if the whole heart of the charity is going to be changed. Everything I believe in has been attacked. The Trustee doesn't know, but by speaking out what he thinks, it has tested me to the core.

He basically said it was wrong to move ahead when our finances are in such a bad way, that it can't be God's best and that we must now change how we operate. In real terms, we should change and become a ministry which responds when the money is in rather than the other way round. This would include not opening any more centres, reducing staff and closing centres where there was insufficient finance within the church. One of his most cutting comments was that he felt the only thing that was distinctive about us, was that we never paid anything on time and were always struggling.

I am numb. The thought of giving up now fills me with pain. I have no real defence apart from FAITH and that's all I've got. In the world's eyes he is right. It looks like foolishness to carry on hiring people and increasing centres when the factual evidence says there is no money.

I will just have to press on and hope God will bring it all through. At the end of the day CAP is his not mine but I will fight every inch of the way to keep the charity true to the foundations God has laid down within us.

November 19, 1999

What a week! I just came out fighting for what I believe is right. Something rose up in me that was from God. I somehow had an authority about what I said. I was so strengthened by God and his word. When I read the scriptures it was as if he had written them just for me – just for this moment.

1 Corinthians 3:10, speaks of the foundation God has laid through me and everyone should be careful how they build on these foundations.

Nehemiah 6:9, says people will say the work will not be completed but I prayed to the Lord 'Now strengthen my hands.'

I Chronicles 11:4, David was told he would not take the city, but he captured the city nevertheless.

Joshua 1:6–9, given to me early in CAP, reads that I should be bold and very courageous, and not depart from his word and I will prosper.

I felt that I needed to state where I believed we were and how we needed to pull together and remain in faith that God was with us. However, I understood that others may not agree and that I needed to know where everybody was at.

During the week I produced a letter and sent it out to all staff and Trustees. All the Trustees and staff have been asked to write to Paul Hubbard (Chairman), with their thoughts. Did they agree with where we were going? Were they willing to stand with me? Did they think we should change?

The initial reaction was one of total support and encouragement. It appears that virtually everybody is with me in how we are doing and it was only this one Trustee who had huge reservations.

I am so pleased with what God has placed within this ministry. We will succeed and press on. I pray that God will bring people to a heart connection.

Praise God for his strength. I somehow know that it's not all over and I know we will be pressed and tested over the coming weeks but with this kind of unity the work will be completed.

November 22, 1999

Over the weekend I received a letter from the Trustee. Quite a difficult letter for me to read. He basically states that he disagrees with how we have developed the ministry and that he does not share my view that we must press on. It's always more difficult to deal with things when they are written down. You find yourself re-reading them.

I agree that if you look with your eyes it looks pretty grim. I say that if you look in faith it looks great. I could not reply to his arguments because logically speaking he was right.

We had a fantastic prayer meeting on Friday. Wonderful words of encouragement and of faith. Everywhere I turn there is encouragement that we are right to just have faith that God will see us through. Not for the first time Word For Today on Sunday was spot on. It said exactly what I've been on about. It even quoted Nehemiah.

Even the Beginner's Bible on Sunday morning TV had me amazed about how faith works against what the world would see. Jesus and the disciples were in a boat during a storm. The disciples thought it would sink and they woke Jesus up. Jesus said that he sent them out in the boat and it wouldn't sink because he was in it! There's also the story of Lazarus who was dead and in a tomb. It looked as hopeless as it can get, yet Jesus raised him to life to show his glory. It's the same with CAP. Jesus sent us out, but he is in the boat so it will not be overwhelmed.

We agreed to press forward and believe that God will vindicate us. We were ultimately to lose one Trustee. To re-read just how God intervened still takes my breath away, and this was in some ways both the lowest and most crucial 'tipping point' of the ministry that I can recall.

The unity and strength of character that was forged in this dark period has laid a foundation of faith, togetherness and a 'nevertheless' spirit that God has used time and time again over the years to bring him glory. The next entry is testimony to people doing extra special things to help us and I pray everyone who helped us, with perhaps no knowledge of our predicament is encouraged by the result. As you will now see after we had made our stand God intervened in the most amazing way. Praise God for his faithfulness.

December 31, 1999

A month of continued pressure and God's intervention. No money came in for the first two weeks and we needed £35,000 to pay November and December's wages and clear our outstanding bills. Then in one week £30,000 came in. Firstly our application to Lloyds TSB came through for £10,000, then I rang Howard Bell, Chief Executive of Provident Financial Plc and asked him if he would let us have the £10,000 they were due to give us in March three months early. He was as always very understanding and after speaking with a couple of the other directors they agreed. Regular giving and one-off gifts began to come in so we were £10,000 short. Then on the Saturday – two weeks before Christmas – I got a Christmas card from a lady who has been wonderful in supporting us over the years, with a cheque for £10,000 in it! Yet again at the very last minute God provided miraculously.

The greatest encouragement over the last month is that we have begun to really push through in our Bradford centre with people getting saved and accepting Jesus as their personal Saviour. Three people got saved in the last month alone and began to have fellowship with us at church. This is what drives us on to press forward because people's lives are at stake. Each one of these people is very precious to God, whatever price we pay they are worth it. I see this as one way the Lord continues to reaffirm that we are in his will.

Wow! What a month and what a turnaround. I believe that through these very difficult three months, God tested our resolve and established a core faith and values within who we are, what we do, why we do it and these core values will continue to bear much fruit.

It seems God really uses these crunch points. They must be a bit like the pain of childbirth. These times are really hard going but they produce good results, bring our goals into sharp focus and help us to learn more of his power.

CHAPTER NINE

CAP AUSTRALIA

APRIL 2000 TO MAY 2000

April 2000

Several months ago I met an Australian businessman visiting the UK. He took some information about CAP and I almost forgot he'd said he would share my work with friends back in Australia.

This man had recently started a company in Bradford and had chosen the same accountants as CAP! He had also picked Trevor Milner as his accountant. (Trevor Milner is a wonderful Godly accountant who looked after CAP's accounts for the first six years.)

He made an appointment to see Trevor and it just happened to be the one after mine. I had left a CAP newspaper for Trevor to read, and he, for some unknown reason left the newspaper on his desk, (anybody who knows Trevor will know of his legendary tidiness and it must have been God for him to leave anything on his desk!). He sat down and picked up the paper and started to read it. He wondered out loud who we were and Graham Newby who was with him, and who knew me through Ruth Graves, said he would bring him to see us. I am amazed at the lengths God will go to bring people together.

Then a fabulous offer came for an all-expenses paid trip for all of us to Australia for a four-week holiday to share the work of CAP with a few people and see if they could duplicate our work there.

Things like this just don't happen to me. All our needs would be met
including spending money, car, a holiday apartment etc.

We were to meet Terry Cahill, and Paul and Linda Scarfe, the pastors of
a church in Cardiff, a suburb of Newcastle in New South Wales. They
were people who we thought might be able to take 'CAP Oz' forward.
Newcastle is a large industrial town two hours north of Sydney. It has
had a declining steel industry and is similar to Bradford in both size
and social demographics.

So off we went, leaving much need at home, but after four years we
needed the break. The first thing to say about Terry Cahill, Paul, Linda,
and their wonderful church the Contemporary Christian Centre
(CCC), is that they delivered everything they said they would.

These people were different. They had a spirit of excellence in all
they did. They did everything they said they would do, right down to
having a car with a child car seat and getting a high chair for Abigail.

Our welcome was wonderful and the way they ministered to us
left a real impression on both Lizzie and myself. I shared the vision
for CAP and they just went for it. I found myself working closely with
them and had to have all our training manuals emailed over. In two
weeks we trained, inspired and equipped them. CAP Australia was
then up and running.

I knew that it would need people of passion, determination and
drive to get this new branch of CAP going. Through prayer and time
with the Lord, I decided to step back a bit when I got back to the UK to
allow them to make it theirs and find their own identity. They did just
that and over the next two years they worked very hard. Their finances
were difficult but in the people close to the work, there was a real sense
of ownership and sowing both financially and in time and effort.

After two years of them testing the procedures and actually
learning how CAP works, I returned in March 2002 on my own for
a whistle-stop two-week visit. I worked with Terry and the team to
help them set up systems so they could expand the work. While I was

there they opened their first two CAP centres, which meant they had three operating when I left. They were such a blessing to me; their enthusiasm, commitment, hard work and their desire to see the lost saved took my breath away.

Several of the "CAP Oz" team have worked with us here in the UK learning more about our systems and procedures and they have very much taken the heart of what we do back to Australia.

It's very rare for a group of people to stretch my faith, but they have a real desire for the lost. I know they will achieve their vision of a CAP centre in every Australian town and city and we will continue to do what we can to help, guide and support them. They are truly a wonderful group of men and women – of character and of God. They have also provided a bridge for CAP to expand into New Zealand.

I find it amazing that God would make something so wonderful happen from a small group of people able to grasp a vision. I pray that the whole CAP Australia team are encouraged by the way they have ministered and encouraged many within CAP in the UK. I am so proud of what they have achieved and so delighted to be able to support such wonderful people. We now have a new management team who have taken on the baton from the original pioneers.

Whichever side of the world CAP is on it is about the same thing, changing lives 'one life at a time'. Here is a testimony from just one of hundreds of people CAP Australia has now helped:

Diane's Story

'After a friend told me about CAP and what they had done for her, I decided to make contact and see if they could help me.

It took quite a while for me to get up the courage to make an appointment to see the centre manager and I was so nervous I considered leaving as soon as I'd got there. My biggest debt was to a loan shark and I was paying him a large amount of interest.

I had been long-term unemployed after bringing up my two daughters Amanda and Erin as a single parent with great difficulty.

Erin had been sick all her life and now has kidney failure. We had many visits to doctors in Newcastle and Sydney and with limited finances I was always struggling to find the fares to get her to doctors appointments.

The difference in my life since approaching CAP has been dramatic. The prayer and encouragement I have received has enabled me to re-enter the workforce which is a major breakthrough. In my previous efforts to increase my income I had taken shift work in Sydney (two-and-a-half hours by train). On one of these trips I was assaulted and because of the fear of attack I was unable to continue commuting. The long periods of unemployment and then the assault had destroyed my self-confidence but I am now back in the workforce in a call-centre and am off all welfare assistance.

I am attending the church where the CAP centre is located and also a mid-week cell with the CAP clients and church members. My daughter Erin has become a Christian through her involvement in the cell and she is enjoying a renewed life.

This year, I went on my first holiday for ages when I attended a Christian Conference in Queensland. The joy of arranging the motel and travel details and then paying for them from my savings, through my CAP budget account was almost as good as the holiday.

I now have confidence as I look to the future as I am debt free, employed and have a network of caring people around me.'

Diane

This testimony could be from anybody here in the UK. There's that same heart, same desperation, same need, same solution and – most importantly – same wonderful outcome.

I can't help thinking back to the word which told me to 'enlarge my tent' back in October 1998. When God gave me the following Scripture I had never imagined he meant 12,000 miles away. But it has become a reality:

"Enlarge the place of your tent, stretch your tent curtains wide, do not hold back: lengthen your cords, strengthen your stakes. For you will spread out to the right and to the left; your descendants will dispossess nations and settle in their desolate cities."

(Isaiah 54:2–3)

CAP Australia is one of those things that is way beyond anything I could ever have imagined in those early and very difficult days. Praise be to God!

The CAP Australia staff team

Ross and Alison Buttenshaw have been a great blessing in both CAP UK and CAP Australia. They came over to the UK in 2003, and we were sorry to see them return three years later. However, they have done so much for the CAP Oz team, taking lead positions and really driving it forward. I am delighted that I still get to work alongside this amazing couple!

CHAPTER TEN

JUBILEE MILL

In September 2000, one of our greatest supporters, Jacqueline, offered myself and three friends her magnificent chateau-cum-castle in Switzerland for three days. We flew to Geneva, rented a car and settled in for what we had thought would be a time of prayer and reflection.

The place was called 'La Lance' and it was a bit like the house in The 'Sound of Music' with a garden sweeping down to lakeside with a jetty and a boathouse. We sailed a beautiful, old wooden sailboat up and down the lake at the bottom of the garden and just had a fantastic time together. There were barbecues on the lakeside, great meals out and trips around the most wonderful Swiss scenery.

One night we were having a meal when I got onto the fact that I was finding it very difficult to raise £250,000 to buy a building for the ever-increasing Bradford based central operation team. We were in an industrial unit and my desk was in a basic breeze-block broom cupboard, and we wanted out! One of my friends said, 'Why don't you use your business skills and put together some business proposal for investors?' We talked about how we could ask several friends with charitable trusts to invest in a building. We could buy the building, and then pay a return on their investment. It would be like rent for us, but we would end up with a great asset for the charity.

With hindsight I think that this was perhaps one of the main reasons we went away. Upon my return I began to think about how and when I could step out in faith and try to find investors and a suitable property.

One man sprang to mind. His name was Bernard and he had a family trust that had supported us with a very large and much needed grant the previous year. I knew he was a very good and sharp businessman and that he would probably be open to such an unusual proposal.

It just so happened that I was due to be staying with him a couple of weeks later and had prepared this amazing presentation about how he might invest some of the money in his trust, get a great return, and help us out. I was sitting at his breakfast table, and I remembered how Nehemiah had asked God to help him when he was about to ask the king for favour. In Nehemiah 2:4, the king asks him, 'What do you want?' Nehemiah just prayed to the God of heaven and spoke out what he wanted.

I just thought 'God will give me the words,' and Bernard asked me what I wanted to ask him. I said, 'Would your Trust invest £150,000 and help me buy a mill to redevelop as a home for CAP?' Before I even had chance to get my presentation out he said, 'Yes!'

I will be eternally grateful for the vote of confidence Bernard showed me then and for his decisive reaction. It was within his power to help and he did not withhold that help. Armed with his support I began looking for a suitable property.

After viewing one small mill, I spotted a billboard out of the corner of my eye on another building. I rang up while we were going back to the office. The young lad at the agents said it was only 8,000 square feet but asked what I wanted. I said I was looking for a large mill that I could develop. He suggested another agent he knew who was selling an old mill through trustees in bankruptcy. I rang up and it was the old Bradford Box Makers Mill just within the inner ring road. It was on the market for £250,000 and was 38,000 square feet, over four floors.

I remember first turning the corner and thinking how beautiful it looked. It was actually a shell of a building that had been abandoned, stripped of everything useful and left to deteriorate. As soon as I walked in I knew this was it. I could see it. God gave me the vision and believe me, it had to be from God. I remember showing other members of the CAP team around and they have since confided in me that they thought I had completely lost my mind. There was so much water on the ground floor you had to wear boots and take an umbrella!

I knew this mill was bigger than the money Bernard said he would lend us. Undaunted, I rang the only other person I knew who might be able to help. This person was Jacqueline, who had lent us her Swiss home a few weeks before. Although I knew her family trust was relatively small, I asked her the same question. Would you believe it, only the week before I rang, there had been a pleasant surprise – the trust had received £50,000 of shares to invest.

Everything was still up in the air but I felt I now needed to press forward and make an offer. I got the figure of just £185,000 to offer to buy it. This meant if we borrowed £235,000, in total, we would be left with £50,000 to start the huge task of beginning the redevelopment.

The agent was flabbergasted by how small the offer was. It worked out at just £5 per square foot to buy – less than many would pay to rent it! A day later he rang back and said the trustee in bankruptcy was very unhappy at my offer, however they would accept it. I rang Bernard up and he agreed to increase the loan to £185,000. When I added the other £50,000 we had enough to buy it and do the immediate repairs and refurbishment to get seven offices for us to move into.

The next few weeks are a complete blur. We had to create loan agreements with undertakings to give the investors a share of the equity we had agreed to return to them. We also asked contractors to quote for the roof, the re-pointing and sandblasting of the walls. Margaret Upstone, who was my PA a the time and a great friend, worked with me and she did the most amazing job. I will never forget standing with Margaret knee-deep in water, with gloves and boots on and ice on the inside of the building, talking to a roofer about getting the roof fixed.

We bought the mill in January 2001. God really moved over the next two months and amazingly we were able to get seven offices ready so we could all move in March. One Saturday we had nearly a hundred people cleaning out the mill. In total we took out ten huge skip loads of rubbish that had accumulated over the past fifty years.

Jubilee Mill: CAP's Headquarters in Bradford

The building was renamed 'Jubilee Mill' after the year of jubilee in Deuteronomy where every seven years, debts were cancelled. Over the last seven and a half years we have seen miracle after miracle. Our plan was to redevelop it in relatively small stages and rent parts out to generate income for future redevelopment and for the charity. In total we raised £1.3 million from supporters, including Kingdom Bank and charitable trusts, some even lending us money interest free, with amounts from £250 to £500,000. With this money, we have redeveloped the mill in its entirety. We faced huge obstacles, ran out of money several times and yet God always provided, albeit sometimes much later than we hoped! We kept a very high standard of refurbishment as anyone who has visited can testify.

We currently use the whole building for CAP's central operations. To walk through this building and see just what God has done is incredible. It is such an amazing resource for the charity, creating an amazing work environment for our staff. To think that over the next five years the entire building will be full of up to two hundred people supporting a nationwide network of centres and changing thousands and thousands of lives everyday is simply fantastic. Jubilee Mill stands as a testimony of what can be achieved when you have a vision from God. When this is combined with people who are willing to step out in faith and do what they can to help, and when you all work hard over a long period of time to a specific strategic plan, you can achieve the unachievable. I would like to thank everyone who made it possible, from the main investors to the people who volunteered to clean out the mill.

One of our greatest gifts in the Jubilee Mill story has been Clive Boldy. Clive was a CAP client who was released from terrible poverty, found Jesus and also led his wife and daughter to the Lord. He is such a humble and hard-working man, whose only desire is to serve God any way he can. He has served us all and CAP very well over five years. His life is one big testimony to God's ability to transform lives.

I want Clive to describe in his own words how Jesus, through CAP, has completely transformed his life.

Clive's Story

'It all started back in 1996, when I took a small loan out for a second hand car. Before that I had hardly ever used credit. I'd never had a car before and the bills just started to come in and very slowly things began to get tighter with our finances. We began to borrow small amounts to repair the car, cover insurance and we also missed one mortgage payment.

Then I borrowed to keep up to date. Before I knew it we were in a spiral of having to borrow to repay ever increasing loans. Suddenly we were very poor.

I worked as an engineer and all my wages were spoken for before I got them. The hot-water boiler packed up and there was just no way I could afford to get it fixed. We went without hot water for two years, with four children aged 14, 13, 11 and 10. It was very hard, especially as my pride would not let me tell anyone or ask for help. We had bought a house back in 1991 in an area that was not that bad, but over the years it began to go down. There were people using and selling drugs outside, meaning the kids and Cath could never go out alone.

We became prisoners in our own home. Even if we could have gone out we never had enough money. We bought the house for £33,000 back in 1991 at the height of the housing boom, but now not only were we falling further and further behind with the mortgage but the house was only worth about £15,000. We still owed over £33,000 and it was going up each month.

My health began to suffer as we were in such a dark place. My only relief was a weekly night out playing darts with my mates. Even then I had to borrow a few pounds for a drink.

After four years of this the crunch came in early 2000. I had a breakdown at work. I was found aimlessly walking around the lathe in a complete daze. People at work were good to me. They drove me home and I just collapsed. Cath phoned the doctor who said I'd had a nervous breakdown. He sedated me and I slept for twenty-four hours.

I knew I had to do something so I went to a company I had seen advertised on the telly. They said they could help, however over the next six months things just got worse. They took our money but my debts just got bigger as they charged and didn't stop interest being added. I also had to still try and pay my mortgage. I was in a desperate situation. What could we do?

Then my sister gave me the most important piece of paper of my life – an information leaflet for Christians Against Poverty offering free debt counselling. Cath phoned and a week later Tim Griffiths (a Bradford Caseworker) came round. After listening to our story and writing down all our information, the first thing he said was that he wanted to pray which I thought was a bit strange. He then worked through all our debts. He took every piece of paper, bills and letters, and told me to leave it with him. If anyone was to ring or more letters came he said to just send them to him. It's impossible to describe just what a relief that was. He said, "Don't worry, we can sort this out if you will work with us." Four years of sheer hell were over. We were not alone and we had hope.

Over the next three months Tim contacted all our creditors and negotiated reduced payments – the results were spectacular. No more letters, no more collectors at our door and no more threatening phone calls. Tim set up a CAP budget account, where all our priority payments such as gas, electric, mortgage, council tax and all the agreed new loan repayments were to be made for us. All we had to do was pay the agreed amount into our budget account each week and we had enough money left to buy food and clothing for our family. What a difference! We even began to save a little and give a few pounds a month to CAP to help others like us.

I was then invited to an evening at John and Lizzie Kirkby's house where I met other people who were in the same boat. I also realised that these Christians were nice people and I started thinking about what life was really all about.

Tim invited me to a Christian basics course run by Christian Life Church in Shipley (the Bradford partner church and where CAP started in 1996), and after three weeks I gave my life to Jesus. Nothing magic happened. It just felt good. It felt like there was something for me to go on for.

I told my work mates I had become a Christian and they ridiculed me and made a massive cardboard cross. I was so elated I just took it off them and put it above my machine. I felt like I was walking on air and nothing could take away the joy I felt inside.

CAP has utterly transformed our lives. With their help we negotiated to leave our home and get re-housed. The building society repossessed our house and sold it for a huge loss leaving me still owing them £24,000. CAP just got stuck in to the building society and eventually they agreed to accept just £1,500 as "full and final

Clive working on top floor refurbishment of Jubilee Mill

settlement" of my total debt of £24,000! What a miracle and that could only have happened through CAP.

My wife, Cath, and my children are all now Christians and we are together as a family at a local church. We also had our first family holiday in 2002, when we went away for a week to Bridlington and we took money we had saved up through our budget account. We had such a great time together as a family. We could afford some treats and the children were really blessed.

In June 2001, I gave my job up to help CAP in Bradford by driving a van to deliver household goods to poor people in the city. I had to take an £8,000 a year wage cut but I still had more money than I had ever had. Within just two weeks of joining CAP an opportunity came for me to head up the redevelopment of Jubilee Mill and I grabbed it with both hands.

Since then my life has continued to be a series of miracles. I have found the right place that God wants me to be. My future is bright and my only goal is to serve my brothers and sisters in this wonderful ministry of CAP. There is no way I could ever repay what they did for my family and me but I will keep trying.

I also want to say a massive thank you to everyone who has ever supported CAP. Without your support CAP would not have been able to help me and I can't even begin to imagine where we would have been now.

Once again thank you CAP and God for my new life.'

Clive Boldy

Jubilee Mill has been such a blessing and I have no doubt we still can't see the real significance of what God has done. It is truly wonderful. We continue to seek land around the building to develop additional car parking. Who knows, maybe we'll have a multi-storey car park in time for the next edition of 'Nevertheless.'

CHAPTER ELEVEN

THE INTERIM YEARS

A s well as developing Jubilee Mill and pioneering CAP in Australia, the work here in the UK continued to grow and develop.

It's important at this time to mention the philosophy we have here at Christians Against Poverty in terms of what we do and how we grow our work. There have been countless headlines and many crucial days and events. But at the end of the day, the real growth of CAP has come simply by devising, developing, analysing and working individually with departments and managers to create opportunities and ensure people are being offered the best service possible. So for these two years we quietly got on with the job.

We saw God intervene in amazing and miraculous ways again and again. One of the most incredible moments occurred towards the end of the interim period, when for the first time ever we were financially up to date by our year end in May 2002.

It started with a simple spreadsheet I did with our Finance Manager. It was February and to our shock it showed that we needed just over £144,000 by our year end in May if we were to finish up to date. This was in addition to all our regular and known gifts.

By April things were getting a bit tight, though we had seen continual miracles of provision and now needed £105,000. But we were actually two and a half months behind with wages and needed £80,000 right then!

I remember actually putting £30,000 on the spreadsheet in absolute belief that a trust I had applied to would give that amount to us.

April 2, 2002

It is eight weeks before our year end. The unthinkable has happened. I've got an awful email from someone I know very well. He's been such a generous supporter over several years.

In paraphrase he says, 'We don't think it's right to give you any money. You are in a mess and need to change what you do.'

It was just a few lines but it was quite harsh. He and his wife genuinely care for me and I know he has written this because he must have honestly believed it was for my good. I am shocked.

I have turned to God's word and asked him for grace to get me through. He has given me Psalm 40. In particular these verses,

> 'Blessed is the man who makes the Lord his trust, who does not look to the proud.'

> (Psalm 40:4a-b)

The following verses summed up how I am feeling.

> 'Do not withhold your mercy from me, O Lord; may your love and your truth always protect me. For troubles without number surround me . . .'

> 'Be pleased, O Lord, to save me.'

> 'Yet I am poor and needy; may the Lord think of me. You are my help and my deliverer; O my God, do not delay.'

> (Psalm 40:11, 13a, 17)

Psalm 41 says,

> '*Blessed is he who has regard for the weak; the Lord delivers him in times of trouble.*'
>
> *(Psalm 41:1)*

As we moved into May 2002, the trustees and senior management team spent an agonising time. Was God telling us to ask the staff to forgo wages? This was such a difficult one so we prayed and sought God. By May 15, with miracle after miracle of money coming in and a really successful mail out to our supporters we were down to needing just £48,000.

Former client, Debbie Thompson, wrote down what she felt the Lord was saying. She had been led to Numbers 20:1-12, and Deuteronomy 32:51. It's the part where the Israelites were in a desperate place and God said speak to the rock. In verse 8, Moses takes matters into his own hands and hits the rock. Water did gush out but God was not pleased because Moses had not trusted and done what God had commanded him to. The consequences of taking things into his own hands were very serious, not only for him but also for the people he led. Later God says to Moses and Aaron,

> '*Because you did not trust in me enough to honour me as holy in the sight of the Israelites, you will not bring this community into the land I give them. These were the waters of Meribah . . .*'
>
> *(Numbers 20:12-13)*

She felt strongly that we should not ask staff to forgo wages and just wait and trust in God. Someone also said, 'Why do we have to get completely up to date for May 31, when we have virtually never been up to date before?' Thank you Josie for that one! However, our accounts are very important for many reasons and we believed it was a godly goal we had prayed about and sought since February.

We were overwhelmed with the amazing outpouring of generosity from our group of supporters. More than five hundred people gave additional gifts. Almost every day we received cheques from a few pounds to a few thousand pounds. Each one came from a person who believed in our vision.

On May 31, 2002 we were just £24,000 short of our target. And by June 14, just fourteen days after our year end, everything was paid.

What an awesome God we have! I praise him for the men and women of God who surrounded me and had the strength to stand against such overwhelming circumstances that said we should cave in.

The results for the year end were astonishing. We had twenty-five centres spread across the country, had helped over 2,500 people during that year alone and seen our income increase to £750,000. However, as year six drew to a close, it became obvious to me and Matt that although everything was really well, it was important that we consolidated what we were already doing.

CHAPTER TWELVE

THE CONSOLIDATION PERIOD:

JUNE 2001 – MAY 2005

As a leadership team we believed that if we simply multiplied what we had by ten, it would be good and would help lots of people. But we really felt that there were things that needed to get stronger and better. We needed to build bigger foundations to see this work really expand. So for the next few years through to the end of 2005, we entered a consolidation period. This was a really important time for the charity and we carried on with what we were doing, pressing forward, growing, building and getting ready for what we knew was about to come.

Matt now explains why we did it, what we did and what happened as a result.

Matt's Explanation

'I love motorways because they are fast and straight. They'll get you there as fast as you can possibly hope for. I have yet to hit that age where going via the A-roads seems a nicer option. Does anyone know when that is supposed to happen? When I look back over the last few years of CAP I believe that we have taken it from being a small windy A-road and turned it into a motorway for the Lord.

The prophet Isaiah declared this:

> 'In the desert prepare the way for the Lord; make straight in the
> wilderness a highway for our God. Every valley shall be raised up, every
> mountain and hill made low; the rough ground shall become level, the
> rugged places a plain. And the glory of the Lord will be revealed, and all
> mankind together will see it. For the mouth of the Lord has spoken.'
>
> (Isaiah 40:3-5)

At CAP we have been in the process of building a highway for one
purpose alone, so that the glory of the Lord will be revealed. God's
glory is forgiveness, it is justice, it is hope, it is mercy, and we are
desperate to see all of those things revealed in the communities he
has called us to.

When John set off back in 1996, he was the ultimate pioneer.
You can just see him wearing a pith helmet with a macheté in his
hand, hacking a path through a jungle. I joined at the point when we
started opening some centres. It was as we opened these centres and
introduced tighter policies and procedures that we effectively upgraded
a rough path to a small road, but still with a number of potholes.

Having spent a few years opening, managing and unfortunately
closing centres, we began to look forward to the future. It was clear
that this road was working. God's glory was being revealed and more
and more families were having their lives transformed. As we looked
towards expansion we started to ask ourselves two key questions.
Firstly, "if we multiplied the centre network by ten, would we be
happy with the quality?" Secondly, "have we got the infrastructure
to handle that expansion?" As we asked these questions we realised
the road needed upgrading for us to successfully expand the work of
CAP across our nation.

From this point, it was clear we needed to evaluate all we were
doing and change certain parts of it. Thankfully this was already so
inherent within the CAP management culture that it was not going
to be a challenge or a big culture shift. In true CAP style we simply

got stuck in. In April 2003, we made a decision to keep the number of centres at thirty-five for the next three years. This would allow us to consolidate and get the road built up ready an increase in serious traffic as new churches came on board and opened CAP Centres.

From a centre perspective there were two elements that we knew needed to improve, the quality of our centres in terms of outputs and the quality of our relationships with churches. At the time our centre network was widely spread in terms of "health." We had some centres that were easily seeing a good number of new clients, were successfully inspiring them to come on board with our service and retaining the clients well, through to the point of being debt free. Alongside this, they were inspiring their churches to get involved, had strong support teams of volunteers and were seeing family after family come to know God and get plugged into the life of the church. They were everything we had dreamed CAP centres could be. In reality however, there was also another end to the spectrum, centres with low client numbers, poor client retention, little church support and no-one coming to faith.

After a lot of prayer, discussion and seeking God, it became clear that in some situations the primary thing that needed to change was the person running the centre. I can remember some of the knots in my stomach when we came to that conclusion for different centres. The centre managers were nice people who I liked, respected and admired but they were just not able to make it work in their situation. To even think about approaching them and suggesting they may not be the right person for the role was horrible. But I do believe that too often in Christian ministry we can be too nice for our own good. We can allow people to carry on doing something instead of biting the bullet and sorting it out.

One of the thoughts that got me through some of these difficult times was that whilst that person stayed in that role they were potentially denying someone who did have the ability to achieve the CAP dream from doing so. How many people weren't being reached?

How many people weren't discovering the life transforming power of the gospel simply because we had the wrong person in the post? I couldn't just sit back and say never mind. I knew it would cause difficulty and I knew centres would shut, but for the people who needed reaching and for the overall health of the charity we had to "bite the bullet."

In the space of one year we closed eight centres and replaced four centre managers in other centres. Every one of them was hard, but in a number of situations it actually revealed that the church wasn't as committed to it as we thought and was simply going through the motions. The lack of prayer and support team was indicative of the underlying lack of support from the church leadership.

There is little point in simply stopping doing something that isn't working, without introducing something that will work, and this is what we did. Throughout this whole process we realised that we needed to establish better, clearer church relationships from day one. We realised the importance of having a senior leader come to visit us in Bradford. We also pinpointed elements in the CAP–church relationship that needed better explanation such as the importance of "Life Changers," and the way we use business practices. At the same time, we also started to present the financial partnership differently and were blown away by the results. In the early days we were delighted when a church agreed to give £6,000 a year towards the work. Yet now we started to see churches stepping out in faith and giving £12,000, £15,000 – even up to £24,000! This made a massive impact on our finances and encouraged us that our church empowering tool was getting more and more effective. The final building block was our "Partnership Agreement" which sets out clearly all the relevant aspects of a partnership prior to a church signing on the dotted line.

The changes we made to our centre network were a really hard grind and in many ways a messy business. However, the changes required to improve our central infrastructure involved a great mixture of creative ideas, new opportunities and entrepreneurial spirit.

Prior to the consolidation period we had identified two key areas that we knew were potentially huge potholes on the road we were building. The first pothole was our physical IT systems managing all of the information on clients' debts, clients' payments and all of the work we had done on each case. The second was that centres were becoming bottle-necked by the administration of clients' debts. They had ever-expanding caseloads to look after and were still trying to see new people.

The problem of systems was the hardest one to solve. I can recall taking a look at another debt agency's software and discussing with their managing director the possibility of us using it. Although the offer was tempting, I knew that we needed to be in control of whatever system we used so that we could present our brand to the finance industry. So in faith I said no to that opportunity, believing that somehow God would meet our needs at the right time in the future.

Bede Feechan joined CAP in January 2001 as a part time Centre Manager in Newton Aycliffe. Bede was flying home from his IT consultancy job in Basingstoke when he first read about CAP in the Daily Express after John won his Tomorrow's People award. Within a few months he had been to visit Bradford with his church leader and was out on the estates of Newton Aycliffe seeing lives transformed before his very eyes.

There is no doubt that Bede was brought for "such a time as this." At head office the systems were starting to creak. We were running over five-hundred accounts using Microsoft Money, which was never designed to take that much information. At the same time Bede was in his centre thinking, "Surely we can do this quicker, faster and with less paperwork."

Out of nowhere Bede offered to write us a system. We then got our heads together to combine his IT expertise and front-line experience with my strategic oversight of the charity's systems to write an exceptional piece of software that has transformed CAP as an organisation.

The HOPE system, "Helping Oppressed People Everyday," combines every element of our debt counselling work. Caseworkers can see on a daily basis if clients have paid into their CAP Account (an account where clients pay a single weekly or monthly amount which CAP can distribute to creditors on their behalf). They can run off reports to highlight those who need a bit of extra support. Information that used to be entered up to three times is now entered just once. HOPE offers a full diary reminder system and a case note system to enable us to easily follow a case history. In addition HOPE has automated all of our banking processes. This has meant that we have been able to increase from £157,000 per month in client payments to £544,000. That's a 246 per cent increase but we have the same staffing levels as we did five years ago. On top of this it was a great personal joy to work with Bede and Ken in Australia to get HOPE re-programmed with Aussie dollars and other technical stuff. We flew out to Australia to implement the system and train the wonderful staff over there in June 2005.

The second pothole was that our centres were being clogged up with too many cases and all of the administration surrounding client debts. Back in 2002 we decided to centralise all our debt negotiations. This involves negotiating with creditors to stop all interest and administrative charges and accept repayment offers in line with the client's budget.

I regularly attended meetings with the credit industry and heard of the difficulties they had with other agencies in terms of contacting caseworkers and also the lack of consistency in the client information they received from them. We realised that if we centralised our debt negotiations we would release our centres from the work, and could provide a massively improved service to creditors and clients. Four years on we have used economies of scale and constant changes to HOPE to keep the staffing levels in our Creditor Liaison Unit (CLU) the same as when we started. This is despite handling £20m of client debt which is rising every month. In addition to this, the great service we provide to the finance industry is reflected in the ever increasing number of companies who give us back ten per cent of all the money we send to them on behalf of our clients.

Two years after starting CLU, we set up our Client Support Unit, which looks after the ongoing elements of a case centrally until a client becomes debt free. They handle everything from clients wanting to withdraw money through to completely re-doing a case if a client's circumstances change. Not only does it provide the client with a better service, because the team are there five days a week instead of being out visiting clients, but it frees up our frontline workers to help more families.

About eighteen months into our consolidation period in November 2004, John and I spent a day evaluating the health of the charity. How was the consolidation period going? How healthy were our centres and how strong was our infrastructure? As we talked it started to become clear that in just eighteen months we had done it, we had achieved what we set out to achieve. CAP was no longer a track, nor was it an A-road. This charity was starting to look like a motorway. It was now ready to take some serious traffic and the infrastructure was in place to support the vision of three hundred centres by 2021. After further input from the senior managers in the charity we took it to the board, and then started making plans to move forward.

Our plans from that time have not changed. We are aiming to open up to twenty new centres per year until we reach a point where every person struggling with debt in the UK can easily access a CAP centre. Since making that decision it has been awe inspiring to see the number of churches streaming through Jubilee Mill, wanting to reach their communities in a relevant twenty-first century way. Although not every church goes on to open a centre, all of them go away inspired by what God can do if we will just trust him and go for his vision with one hundred per cent of what we have to give.

As we reflect on all that has been achieved and press on to achieve the goal, it's important to remember that it is simply about changing one family and one life at a time. We must stay connected to God's heart for broken people. At our annual staff conference in June, I listened as Caseworkers shared stories of some of the most horrendous broken lives that they have been called to minister to over the last year. I just felt each one cutting me deeper. I felt overjoyed that they had happy endings and that we as CAP had managed to transform their lives. But as God's spirit touched me I just started to cry and was sobbing like I hadn't for years, from deep within as I felt some of the pain of the lives we had touched. Even more than that, I thought of those we hadn't reached, those who did not know the love, joy and peace of knowing God and I cried for them. It is for each and every one of them that we have done the above. It is for them and because of God's heart of compassion within us that we will simply press on to see every person in the UK have access to the amazing work of Christians Against Poverty and see thousands of people come to know Christ.'

Matt Barlow

CHAPTER THIRTEEN

THE END OF THE BEGINNING

JANUARY TO MAY 2006

As we pushed through to the end of our first ten years, it was obvious to me that this was the end of the beginning. This is where we finished after ten years, but don't forget this is only the start of another amazing ten, twenty, and one hundred years of CAP. Fasten your seat belts because you're in for a bumpy ride.

Tuesday January 3, 2006

As I look out of my office here in Jubilee Mill I am struck by how much God has achieved over the last nine and a half years. This coming year will be another amazing one for us. We will grow from thirty-six centres to over fifty, and see literally thousands of lives transformed. Maybe 300 people will make first time commitments to Christ. This year will have its fair share of struggles, difficulties and great breakthroughs like all the years before! For me it will be the end of ten glorious years of personal struggle to get this amazing work of God established.

Over the last few months I have felt that I needed to hand over the day to day control and management of CAP UK to Matt Barlow. Matt has been with me for seven years and is my right hand man. As Operations Director he has steered us through the last few years and is a skilled manager and great leader. I sense

143

I need to pass CAP UK over to him and move myself into a very important supportive role here in the UK. This will also create space for me to develop CAP internationally.

It's new and exciting! However, there is no doubt that I do feel the weight of the decision. It is hard to pass something on that has been very much your life for ten years. Yet there is something deep within me that says I need to do it for CAP to move to the next level. I don't feel like I am stepping down, just stepping up and aside to let Matt take the helm.

Matt and I have worked on our new roles. We have such a great relationship and a trust that God is ultimately in charge. I know that any authority I have is from God and my whole journey since CAP began has been one of delegation and development of others. It's just a bit strange when the reality hits you that you are about to delegate the running of CAP UK.

Tuesday January 11, 2006

We are about to go away for three days with twenty of our department managers, area managers and the senior management team. We really appreciate these times when we can inspire, train and build a real team approach to our vision and strategy.

I will be sharing with them my decision to become International Director and Matt's promotion to UK Chief Executive and my role of supporting him. I feel that once I have spoken this out it's a done deal, and although I know it's right to step aside I do feel somewhat anxious.

Monday January 16, 2006

We had a great three days last week with the managers. The response to my announcement was tremendous. Virtually the whole team spoke to me and were so encouraged and amazed that I had done what I had done. Matt was great and said some fantastic stuff about me. The whole three days were amazing and the managers are buzzing this morning. I am just amazed with the group of people God has brought around me. As a group they are going to change the world, and as a team they have and will achieve so much more than I ever could on my own.

At this point I just want to share with you Matt's thoughts on taking over this vital role of UK Chief Executive.

Matt's Thoughts

'Over the last few years, John has gradually empowered me to lead more and more of the charity. It has been my privilege to do that and release him to do what only he can do. Despite that it was still quite a shock when in November 2005 John asked me to take over the formal leadership of CAP UK as Chief Executive.

After a lot of thought, prayer and discussion, it became clear that I needed to do this for a bigger purpose. I could see that the UK foundations were laid. We knew where we were going and how we were to get there. John's unique pioneering gifting was needed elsewhere. Just as much as the UK needs CAP, there are other nations where the disadvantaged are getting caught up in the web of debt and they need the church to rise up and meet those needs. John needs to be released into the unknown, to create some space to enable CAP to flourish internationally. Me taking over as Chief Executive in the UK would facilitate that. I can also see that the blend of gifts that God has given me fits perfectly with leading and growing CAP in the UK, both as a movement and as an organisation. God had seen this time coming before I even started at CAP, and it's with great humility that I take hold of God's call and now run to see this vision come to pass. John will remain at my side and I appreciate his ongoing commitment to supporting me and CAP UK.

One of the biggest blessings in my life as a Christian has been to work alongside John Kirkby since 1999. John is the most amazing leader. The fact that I have worked "alongside" John, not "under" him is a great testimony to his humble heart and empowering spirit. John amazingly combines a real pioneer gifting with a true bulldog spirit. He does life fast and he does life big. You truly know when you've met John, he's so full of faith and passion. Yet at the same time, I know few people who are so humble and so open to my thoughts, opinions and from time to time even correction. I have learned probably ninety per cent of who I am as a leader from John and for that I will be eternally grateful.'

Matt Barlow

Tuesday January 17, 2006

All systems go and I'm very busy working with Matt on the budget for our next financial year. It's really encouraging to see him planning what we need to spend and not holding back because we have no money.

Every month I send out a mid-month financial update for staff and here is today's:

From: John Kirkby
Sent: 17 January 2006 10:47
To: All CAP Staff
Subject: Finance Update

Hi CAP team

I sense quite a challenging few days and weeks ahead of us regarding our financial situation. We need £52,000 to be able to pay the balance of November salaries and have £38,000 available for on time salary requests. As I sit here today we have no indication where any of this money will come from which means we are, as always, totally reliant on God. Please email your salary needs to Lydia by 10:30am on Monday 23 January. We will then update everyone with our current financial situation.

It is obvious to me that we do need a large financial injection over the coming few weeks, however, we are continuing to press forward with all the preparation for new centres and other infrastructure in faith that God will provide.

Let's be diligent in making our requests known to God as it says in Philippians,

'Don't worry about anything; instead, pray about everything. Tell God what you need, and thank him for all he has done. Then you will experience God's peace, which exceeds anything we can understand. His peace will guard your hearts and minds as you live in Christ Jesus.'

(Philippians 4:6-7)

John

I've just received the finance report, which predicts expenditure and any income expected. It also gives me various figures such as how much we need to pay estimated on time salary requests. The report also shows me how much we need to get completely up to date to pay everyone and all our bills. This month is a record! We need a staggering £177,123.55 to get everything paid by the end of January. It's been the same ever since we started! God has simply encouraged me to believe that he has everything in his hands and all I need to do is stand firm.

Today we sent in our bid for some government money through a combined bid with other Christian organisations. We have had such a battle to be included. Our radical approach to working with churches, being Christian, evangelistic and a determination that we will do the work even if we don't get the £730,000 two year grant really freaks people out. Praise God for Keith Tondeur from Credit Action and Malcolm Duncan of Faithworks who stood by us and supported our inclusion. We all stopped and prayed over the application and committed it to God. We find out in April so there is nothing we can do other than pray. We are also waiting to hear from another Foundation to see if we have been awarded a £200,000 grant over two years.

It's important to understand that we don't wait for the money before we step out in faith, we simply step out believing God will provide for us. This year we expect to have approximately fifty centres by September and our budget for our next financial year starting on June 1, will be approximately £2.5 million. We will simply carry on with the vision God has given us.

It's so important for people to know that we are not built on huge grants but that everything we are sent makes a real difference. Every penny given regularly through our 'Life Changer' programme is really needed. I pray our supporters will understand how vital they are to seeing God's vision become a reality.

At the end of the day, the one thing of eternal value is that four clients got saved on that day. Every week we get stories from our centres for our weekly praise and prayer report. I just wanted to include the following emails for you to sense just how much we value our clients and how important each of the lives we work with is.

From: CAP Centre Manager
Sent: 17 January 2006 12:07
To: John Kirkby
Subject: Salvation!

Salvation!! This couple came on board as clients a few months ago. She was very depressed when I met her and under great stress dealing with work, home and children. Recently she has had to give up work. Her support worker and I have been helping her and this Sunday was her second visit to the church where the words spoken in the service moved her to tears. We prayed with her, sharing the Gospel again and she asked Jesus into her life! So amazing! Immediately we saw such a difference in her face. She was no longer frowning but smiling!! Please continue to pray as she steps out on her road to freedom in Christ!

CAP Centre Manager*

From: CAP Centre Manager
Sent: 17 January 2006 12:07
To: John Kirkby
Subject: Salvation report

Praise God! Susan Sadler (Evangelism and Discipleship Manager), did an evangelism evening here on Saturday and a young girl gave her life to the Lord. On the way home in the car her friend (who became a Christian on the Discovery Break) kept telling her how wonderful Jesus is. She said, 'He never leaves you and he is always there for you to talk to.'

CAP Centre Manager*

Thursday January 19, 2006

Things are really getting going in lots of areas. I spent some time with Matt looking at the budget proposals for 2006–07 and we are faced with a huge decision. In short, we need in the region of £2.5m in our next financial year if we go for everything we feel we need to see the work expanded to over 60 centres by May 2007.

It seems so surreal speaking about setting a budget which requires £700,000 income above our expected regular income when we need £177,000 today to be up-to-date. We also interviewed three new centre managers today for new centre openings in April. Just like the first managers in October 1998, we have no money to pay existing staff yet we are still pressing forward.

3:30pm
I got a phone call from a friend whose trust has supported us over the last few years. He basically said that they would help us raise £250,000. They agreed to give us £62,500 on a match

funding basis (i.e. if I can get three other people to give £62,500
or somehow raise £187,500.)

This awesome thing really encourages me that God can
provide for us and I am inspired to start asking the few people I
know who might be able to help.

Friday January 20, 2006

No money came in today and we now have the on-time salary
requests from Monday. We need a minimum of £37,000 and
have no idea where it's coming from. Matt and I spent a short
time discussing what to do and basically we reached our usual
conclusion, carry on today. It's not over until Monday mid morning
and it's up to God. This is the kind of faith CAP operates in and is
really quite frightening, yet somehow I feel peace in my heart. We
have been here for the last nine and a half years and God's not
changed his mind, we will get through and he will get the glory.

Monday January 23, 2006

12:30pm

I've just finished a meeting with Matt Barlow and the finance
team. We need £33,000 to be able to pay on-time requests and
the balance of November's salary. Matt and Josie, and Lizzie and
I have a combined £42,000 in our banks for a short period of time
due to moving house, re-mortgaging and selling our properties.
We have decided that we will lend CAP the money.

None of us could stand by and see staff not paid. We are
totally confident that God will provide over the next few days,
weeks or months. Matt said it all when he basically said any
blessings we have and any cash God happens to bring to us is
all his anyway. Let's just believe there is a massive outpouring of

finance just around the corner and what a privilege it is to stand side by side with the staff.

I have just sent the following email to staff.

From: John Kirkby
Sent: 23 January 2006 12:13
To: All CAP Staff
Subject: Financial Update

Hi CAP team

Well the day has come and although we received a couple of thousand pounds this morning we are well short of the amount needed to clear November and pay on time salary requests. We were offered loans from three members of staff who miraculously had some money available and after due consideration we have accepted the loans. This means that we are able to pay the salary requests – they will be paid today.

We are all confident that God will, over the next few days and weeks, release some substantial funding towards the charity. We have loads of possible ways by which he could provide for us, and at the end of the day we have to do what we have to do.

Please keep praying and seeking God for a miraculous and large financial injection into the charity over the coming few days and weeks and let's rejoice that we have managed to meet all our needs although we would have preferred it another way.

Thanks for your continued faith and support as a team. We really have all pulled together and it will be such an amazing time when we are able to celebrate what God will do as I remain as confident as ever that God will see us through.

Come on God!!!

John

Tuesday January 24, 2006

We finished the financial and strategic plan for June 1, 2006 to May 31, 2007. Matt has done such a great job in bringing this document together. We really are going to build this massive network of centres based in local churches - you can feel the faith rising and the strategy becoming clear. I am going to ring two more potential large donors when I work late tonight.

Two people were saved today and there are great testimonies of how God has reached out to these people. Here's the email.

From: CAP Centre Manager
Sent: 24 January 2006 14:33
To: John Kirkby
Subject: Salvation!

Hi CAP team

Get that bell rrriiiiiinngggiiiinngg! We had a salvation today! Praise God! A few weeks ago this client called telling us her husband had just walked out on her and that divorce proceedings had started. The Holy Spirit encouraged me to ask her to come to church on Sunday and I offered a lift. She declined the lift, but on Sunday she very bravely and nervously came.

She absolutely loved it! Unfortunately, due to other commitments she had to leave early. Anyway, our first visit was today. When we turned up, you could sense the Holy Spirit.

Very early in the conversation we talked about Jesus and you could tell she was open (plus she had all her paperwork ready and had done all the things that I had asked her to do). After the conversation we talked some more and I told her the gospel. I asked her if she wanted

Jesus to be her Saviour and there was a resounding yes. I showed her the prayer in the 'Why Jesus?' booklet and we prayed it together. After the prayers she virtually grabbed the booklet from us saying, 'Can I have this?' I also left her a book and will be giving her a Bible.

She was obviously hungry. She apologised for not coming last Sunday and said that she's coming this Sunday and 'Can I bring a friend?' Flip me! She can bring a hundred! Please pray for her protection and for her growth. She's taken a huge step into freedom today! Praise God!

CAP Centre Manager*

When the centre manager mentions ringing a bell, they are referring to an old fire bell we have in Jubilee Mill that we ring every time anyone is saved as a direct result of our work. All Bradford staff stop work and gather to pray for the newly saved person. It's a real reminder to the Bradford staff (who don't see clients) just why we do what we do. Over recent months we have been 'disturbed' up to three times a day! Praise God!

Wednesday January 25, 2006

Will today be the day we receive a huge cheque or will it be another day of simply pressing forward and doing our job? Who knows! But I am sure God is in charge. Will anyone be saved today?

Just had morning prayers where we spend the first fifteen minutes together every day praying as a staff team. Wednesday is our weekly bulletin morning where we get an update of some of the stuff that's happened over the last week.

I got an incredible sense of God's presence in what we do and an overwhelming sense within my spirit that he just has to provide for something that represents his heart for people as much as we do. CAP is his, it's not ours. He will provide for what he has intended, I really can relax and just go with God's flow.

Thursday January 26, 2006

It's 10:45am and I've just been told that a large foundation has said no to our grant application for £200,000 that I mentioned a couple of weeks ago. It was a nice letter showing that they had obviously thought through our proposal, but they think our plans are too ambitious and don't seem to understand exactly what we do. We could not have done a better application and although I always knew it would be a long shot I do feel quite devastated. If they had agreed to £100,000 a year for two years it would have been such a help and such an encouragement for us all. As it is we just feel flat. Why is it so hard? Why do we get rejected so many times? Why not the big breakthrough? We step out in faith, believe, stand strong, do everything we can – we just need a massive miraculous breakthrough. I have expectant faith and I really did think this would be the one, yet it's not. There is a definite B-side to expectant faith, it's called disappointment and it hurts!

The whole team, although disappointed, show their usual resolve to simply carry on doing what we do and believe God is in control. I really appreciate that my relationship with God is real and that he allows me to be genuinely upset and vocalise with him when I feel let down.

I pray, 'O God, please help us over the coming few days and weeks. I know you will get us through, but I still find it hard when we seem so under funded and still, after nearly ten years of struggle and difficulty, are unable to pay staff on time or have to borrow money to do so. Come on God, please help!'

11:30am

I've just been round the departments here in Jubilee Mill telling them the news. What an amazing bunch of people they are, wanting just to support me and pull together. It is such a joy to see people who probably have not been paid standing in faith and strongly believing that God will provide.

Clive Boldy had a word for me this morning.

> *'O love Jehovah, all you saints of his; Jehovah preserves the faithful, and abundantly repays the proud doer.'*
>
> *(Psalm 31:23)*

What a word on such a day as this, 'O God please preserve us this day and abundantly repay us as we continue to be doers of your will.'

2:15pm

In the midst of today I receive this email:

> **From:** CAP Centre Manager
> **Sent:** 26 January 2006 14:01
> **To:** John Kirkby
> **Subject:** Amazing salvation
>
> Hi CAP team
>
> Salvation of client's daughter. She had lost her children because she was in a violent relationship and on drugs. She was resistant to the gospel and the changes that have taken place in her mum. She walked into church after the meeting on Sunday and asked for help wondering whether God would accept her after all she had done. Of course the answer is yes.
>
> CAP Centre Manager*

This is what it's all about.

Tuesday January 31, 2006

At 10:30am our winter conference will be starting. We have one hundred and fifteen people coming including all staff plus some support workers and prayer team co-ordinators. This is such a vital time for us. We will use the next two days to inspire and support them, give information and generally draw us all together.

Obviously this is against the backdrop of our financial difficulties, although the atmosphere in prayers this morning was great. It was my turn to lead and I just focused us all on how amazing God is.

The Management Board meeting was yesterday. Although it went well in many ways, it revealed some insecurity in me, which I didn't like. It's hard when you feel people have not recognised the enormity of Matt taking over as Chief Executive, and I feel a sense of being a little taken for granted and not as encouraged as I could have been. I do however realise that it's God who is my encourager as well as many of the staff around me. I am determined that I will not lose the joy of the next two days. Having our insecurities revealed and dealing with them is always a good thing even if it feels pretty bad whilst it's happening.

Tuesday February 7, 2006

Things continue to be very up and down. I'm doing lots of work with Matt and the guys to get the next eight centres ready to be opened in April. We have five agreed now which is fantastic. There were some great testimonies over the weekend, with eleven people saved in one of our CAP centres!

> **From:** CAP Centre Manager
> **Sent:** 07 February 2006 09:52
> **To:** John Kirkby
> **Subject:** Salvations, Salvations, Salvations!!
>
> Eh up crazy CAP crew in Bradford,
>
> Ok I know this is going to be a long one for the bulletin, but we had eleven salvations on Saturday when Susan Sadler came to speak to us. Praise God!!! The training in the morning was great and with the social afterwards, including kids, there were about forty CAP clients. We had some food; there was giant Jenga, scalectrix, bouncy castle, etc. Then Susan gave a talk. One of my clients gave their testimony and Susan did an altar call. Suddenly, loads of people broke into tears and they and their families gave

their lives to Jesus – it was just amazing. You could see healings happening and God's Spirit breaking into people's lives. My church leaders are planning on rolling out Saturday afternoon discipleship parties every three weeks to cater for them.

I could go on about how great a day it was. I haven't slept since – have been too excited. Please thank our awesome God for this and pray for these seeds to be watered.

CAP Centre Manager*

Wow!

Wednesday February 8, 2006

Matt has been working with Janice looking at our total financial needs for the remainder of this year. This is always a challenging thing to do as it really highlights your needs.

The actual figures bring home to me just how utterly reliant on God we still are. We need £147,129 by the end of February to get completely up to date and then, allowing for all expenses and regular income plus all known donations, we will need another £292,577. That's £439,706 in total.

This amount would pay every bill, every wage, all the expenses associated with opening the eight centres in April, and would mean that after ten years we would be straight. What a thing that will be when it happens. All that faith, struggle, perseverance and sheer desire to press forward all vindicated by God.

I have just received the following email from one of our centre managers, which says it all. This struggle is worth it and so many lives are being changed by what we do. God simply must provide all we need.

From: CAP Centre Manager
Sent: 08 February 2006 10:00
To: John Kirkby
Subject: New salvation

Phoned new client to see how she was to find her very upset. Her daughter had told her that she was no longer needed to look after her granddaughter over the weekends. I prayed for her over the phone and she said she felt so much better for it. I asked her if she had read the 'Why Jesus?' booklet I had given her. She said that she had read it and had asked Jesus to come into her life. Fantastic! I said that she needed to go to church and suggested her boss's church as he introduced her to CAP and the church he attends is close to where she lives. She said that was a good idea and that she would do so. Please pray that she will grow in God's love.

CAP Centre Manager*

Monday February 13, 2006

This morning Matt and I brought the reality of the financial position to the managers and department heads. They were really positive and encouraging. It's such a joy to see so many people with the same heart and determination to get through. Everyone seemed cool about the way we intend to move forward next year with everyone supporting the decision to step out in faith with a budget of £2.5m. They all understand that the amount of faith required is massive, and it's great how they really do trust Matt and me with this.

Tuesday February 14, 2006

Big meeting this morning when we repeated the situation with all the staff. We actually videoed it so centre staff could see us and get the same message. Again, a fantastic response, they really did seem to rise to the challenge.

We also announced about the trust that had agreed to give us £62,500 if we could raise the remainder of the £250,000 from other sources. This obviously helped raise our spirits, and

I do pray that these generous people will know just what their amazing support means to the whole CAP team and me.

Friday February 17, 2006

I just spoke with Matt from London. We had to discuss what to do on Monday about the on time salary situation. The bottom line is grim. By Wednesday next week we will be in a very big hole financially. The only thing I can do is re-lend the £25,000 Lizzie and I have from our house move, which was intended to pay off the costs of building work on our new home.

I just don't think I can leave the staff not paid when we can do something.

'O God, when will it all end? What are you doing, why is it so hard? I am really finding this time very challenging, my emotions are stretched and raw, I'm tired and weary of it all. I am no superman and really do feel the weight. It's when I am weak that you are strong. I feel very lonely in the face of such pressure.'

The problems we face will pass, they always do and always have, yet I am not immune to the pressure and sense of severe difficulties. I suppose God has been preparing us all for such a time as this for nearly ten years, but it's still not easy. Praise God that I can simply rest in his arms and just know that he is in control.

Sunday February 20, 2006

Lizzie and I have spent the weekend thinking, praying and talking about what we should do on Monday morning regarding the massive needs we have. I have been taken back to May 2003, when we were in a difficult situation not dissimilar in magnitude to our present one. I was led then, and returned this weekend, to Numbers 20:9–12 and also the connected verses in Deuteronomy 32:51. It's where Moses hits the rock and water comes out, yet God was not pleased because he had simply told Moses to speak to the rock, not hit it.

The context of the passage is that Moses was in a real place of pressure. He faced insurmountable odds and I think his sheer desperation and frustration at his circumstances, and maybe with God, made him hit the rock. Although God did the miracle and water did gush from the rock, it's clear that God wanted Moses not to even touch the rock. I feel that was to make it absolutely clear that God made the miracle happen, not Moses.

This has led us to the conclusion that it's not a time for us to lend this money to CAP. We simply need to pay for our building work and as it were, 'speak to the rock.' It's in God's hands now. The amounts we need are so big even our £25,000 would only delay the reality for a few days. We have decided to allow God to work the miracle. After talking with Matt, I have decided to sit down with the senior team on Monday morning and let all the staff know we have actually run out of money and simply give it over to God. I can't carry it any more it's just too big. We have cleared all our outstanding building work costs on time this afternoon so there is no way back for us - it's God or nothing!

Monday March 6, 2006

We are in real financial difficulty right now. We need £65,000 by Thursday to pay the balance of December's salaries and our outstanding bills. In total, we need £261,340 to get up to date and repay the short term loans from last month. Although I am aware of the difficulties, I feel quite calm about the situation. God will get us through and although it's hard for everyone, we either believe he is in control or we don't.

I am just reading a great book called The Leadership Secrets of Saint Paul by Jeff Caliguire. He talks about what Paul says in Philippians,

'For I have learned how to get along happily whether I have much or little. I know how to live on almost nothing or with everything. I have learned the secret of living in every situation, whether it is with a full stomach or empty, with plenty or little. For I can do everything with the help of Christ who gives me the strength I need.'

(Philippians 4:11-13)

Over the last nine years I have learnt how to just get along and enjoy the ride. It encourages me that the apostle Paul, who had a God inspired life mission also had times when he had no food. The biggest gift is the ability to remain positive in the face of such difficulties. I am so aware of God being with me and that without his grace there is no way I could stand at this present time. Nevertheless, with his spirit inside us, we can withstand so much and I remain certain that by May 31, 2006, God will see us through. There is a miracle to come that will astonish even me. (I just pray it comes soon!)

The bell just went and we heard of three clients saved in Scarborough over the weekend. What great encouragement, today of all days to see that God is doing his stuff. I also received notification that we have five churches confirmed for an April centre opening, with another two only needing the people to be interviewed. How great it is that whilst faced with such difficulties we are still pressing forward with the vision, Plan A and no plan B!

Tuesday March 7, 2006

I sat all the staff down in Bradford and explained our current serious financial situation. I really felt it was right to keep everyone up to date and that the truth is very important. We are not trying to 'spin' stuff, we simply deal with the reality of the situation we face.

I sent the following email to all staff which explained where we actually are this morning.

From: John Kirkby
Sent: 07 March 2006 09:44
To: All CAP Staff
Subject: Financial Situation

Hi team

Well the moment we all hoped would not come has arrived in so much as at this precise moment in time we have reached a point where we have no money to be able to pay any further salary requests. We need to apply our known regular income to pay the remaining requests received at the end of last month together with the outstanding December salaries. We also need to pay all outstanding bills which we are able to do. Until the situation improves there is no money to pay anyone.

I know for the vast majority of you this financial reality may well be a new experience, and I want to reassure you all that we understand just how difficult this will be for many of you. Not only practically but also from a spiritual point of view. Having been here before, although not often to this extent, my only words of advice are that you should share your disappointment with God and continue to believe that God will see us through and simply stand in faith for your individual needs. It's as if we signed up for it, we knew it was always a possibility, we sing about it, read about it but the reality is pretty grim to actually live through.

We are doing all we can, and our strategy remains the same. To simply continue with what God has directed us to do. I have no doubt God will see us all through and that he is in control and knows best. Even though I think he should release loads of money today I am willing to bow to his sovereign hand and ultimate control.

It's important that we don't lose sight of all God has, is and will do, and that we remain focused on presenting our requests to him. I remain confident, despite huge factual evidence to the contrary, that God will provide and that by the end of May we will all see a miracle in our finances.

I am so proud of you all and remain humbled that God would allow me to lead the charity at a time such as this.

John

I received the following email from Claire Kempster, who has only been with us a few months. It really encouraged me that God has really birthed something in the people who work here.

From: Claire Kempster
Sent: 07 March 2006 11:32
To: John Kirkby
Subject: Financial stuff

Hey John,

Just wanted to encourage you by saying that although the prospect of not having money is a difficult thing for me, I came into this job expecting this situation to happen within the first year!

Now, I'm not saying I have no faith in your leadership and the way CAP is run, but I'm saying that being tested by God like this is something that I took as being a standard clause in God's version of my CAP employment contract! It's something that although a bit scary, has in no way knocked me sideways, as my heart was totally prepared for this situation to arise.

I don't believe it's God's will for CAP to remain in this situation any more than you do, but I know that he has a plan, a perfect plan – and this season is part of it. The beautiful thing about seasons in the natural is that they last just long enough for you to appreciate them – just when you start to get fed up with driving to and from work in the dark during winter, the days start to get longer again. It's the same in the spiritual – just when we feel we can't take anymore trouble, or just when we start to lose momentum because everything seems so easy, God sends a new season to change our perspective of things. God's a bit clever like that, you see!

I might be a little bit weird, but I'm almost excited by this situation because of the amazing miracle I know God will perform. How much rejoicing will that bring into the building when it arrives, eh? For now, chin up and just keep trusting, right?

Claire

I continued to get loads of similar emails over the next few days, all really supportive and full of faith.

Tuesday March 14, 2006

Today the reality of our situation continues to really hit home. I was told by one of my most supportive and committed managers that some of her staff had expressed real difficulties in both living with and understanding our current situation. I know that there will be others who feel like this. It's totally understandable and whilst I agree with their thoughts, I'm confused and upset as well. To hear that people who need to be paid are simply unable to manage is really hard for me to take. I just want to encourage and support them but I realise that it's just one of those times when I have to let people work things through with God. I can't offer anything else but faith and my determination to do what I can do to get us through. It's hard when you realise just what the consequences of having no money are for staff.
I have had to just steady myself today and remind myself of all the promises God has made us. The pressure is growing and every avenue I have tried has come to nothing.

However, I got three emails from pastors of partner churches saying they would advance their next few monthly contributions if that would help. Also a great mate of mine said he would bring his increased regular gift forward to start 1 April. These are all drops in the ocean but really important to me.

Thursday March 16, 2006

What a morning!!

At 9:30am, a member of staff called to see me. He said he and his wife had decided to donate £62,500 from the proceeds of a pending house sale to the charity! He said God had told him a few weeks ago but had asked him not to say anything to me until he was released to by God. He said when he heard me speak this morning he felt God say, 'tell him today.' Although it will take up to three months to be released, it still makes a huge difference to how I feel.

Praise God for his amazing unexpected provision. I sent an email to the Management Board letting them know and I decided not to say anything to anyone except Matt until Monday. I just sensed that by then God would have done something more and that leaving people to stand for the next few days was right. I am also aware that in practical terms nothing changes because we still have no actual money to pay any wages.

Monday March 20, 2006

As I was seeking God about what to do this crucial week I felt him say to me, 'Concentrate on what you need right now, don't worry about the overall amount – I have that in hand.' I looked at our needs this week and came to the conclusion that if we actually had the £62,500 promised gift from the member of staff we would be able to make a serious attempt at paying staff's urgent needs.

I then worked through some options and felt prompted to take the opportunity to get staff involved. I sent an email and contacted the Management Board with a proposal asking staff if they wanted to loan money, short-term, interest free.

I also had a great phone call with my mate I met last week who said he really wanted to help and was willing to come from London to spend Wednesday with us.

Tuesday March 21, 2006

I sent the following email:

> **From:** John Kirkby
> **Sent:** 21 March 2006 10:13
> **To:** All CAP staff and management board.
> **Subject:** Financial update
>
> Hi team
>
> The situation continues to unfold daily. Yesterday we received confirmation of unexpected £9,000 trust gift money in over next two weeks. Just this morning we received a £500 staff gift, plus £1,500 from completed insolvency IVA work and £1,000 in general gifts. This brings the total received since we started our target of £439,000 four weeks ago to £48,500. We also received news that a member of staff is to donate £62,500 to the charity and that this money will be with us by the end of May. That's £111,000!! Praise God for this staff member's faithfulness and their amazing generosity; real Acts 2 stuff!! (Acts 2 is where people sold land and gave money to the Apostles to distribute to the poor.)
>
> So what do we do now? Well I am continuing to talk and share our needs with various supporters and it's starting to bear fruit although nothing is concrete right now. The issue is that we still do not have the actual funds to make any salary payments this week, however I sense God has given me a strategy that enables us all to get involved and will

really honour our corporate heart of faith and support for each other.

I felt God saying to me earlier this week that I should concentrate on the current needs and I realised that if we had the £62,500 promised gift today we would be able to make some much needed salary payments by the end of the month. In consultation with the management board we have decided that we want to give everyone at the heart of the ministry a chance to get involved themselves by asking everyone to consider lending the charity money, interest free which we will repay when the £62,500 gift is received by the end of May. We feel it's really important everybody knows that the amount is not important, it's taking part that's the great opportunity. Like the young boy with his loaves and fishes he brought what he had, God did a miracle and there was enough for all who had need and there were twelve baskets left over!

Because time is pressing please email Janice with the amount you can lend, asap, and send the cheque for her attention as soon as possible and we will send you a receipt and confirmation of repayment by May 31, 2006. I also want everyone to send Lydia your precise salary needs over the next two weeks up to 5 April. Please give the exact amount you need and the date you need it in your bank. Obviously the later the better and I need to re-emphasise that at this moment we have nothing to pay anything, it's just presenting our request to God, stepping out in faith and giving us some idea of what we need and when we need it.

So why ask people to lend instead of simply forgoing your own salary? The answer is that by doing it this way we are responding corporately and it is an extension of our faith to lend money hoping and believing that as a combined group we will raise enough for all our combined needs instead of individually using our own money to see us through. It's like the young boy with his two fishes and five loaves; he could not have given his dinner and eaten it himself. Yet by handing what he had over in faith for his own needs both he and everyone else got what they needed – everybody won through his generous heart. That's why it's vital we all get involved and although I know and appreciate many of us have used savings and forgone wages over the last few months, I really sense in my spirit this is a moment, an opportunity for us to draw together. I want to re-emphasise that my faith remains strong that God will get us through in the same way as when Jesus was challenged about why he was 'late' when Lazarus had died. Jesus replied, 'So my glory would be known.'

Thank you so much for your amazing trust, support and sheer strength of character to stand at a time such as this. I know God is delighted by your faith and our corporate steadfast determination to press on. God's glory is being shown daily.

John

I find it hard to explain what I'm feeling right now but it's excitement, mixed with fear, mixed with peace. What will the next few days bring?

Wednesday March 22, 2006

8:15am

Came in early today, just needed a few moments with God. I really sense that we are coming to a pivotal few hours and days. I was astonished to find that staff have already pledged £47,000 in interest-free loans. The largest was £30,000 the smallest just £20, yet I know both come from a heart to bring their 'loaves and fishes.'

Let's believe the next three days are the amazing days I have been waiting for, and that they are the beginning of a most incredible end to ten of the most challenging years of my life. I feel so calm and content. Praise God for his grace and love just when I needed it most.

9:40am

I had a very moving moment this morning. A lady who works for us as a volunteer, and who is a former client, has just come into my office saying that her husband worked overtime for the last two weeks and they want to give us £100 of the £200 earned. I am almost in tears just thinking of their heart for us. She said, 'We've only just found out how tight it is and want to help where we can.' God is amazing; in the midst of such a day he brings this gem to encourage me.

Thursday March 23, 2006

9:00am

Yesterday my mate from London who I visited on 15 March came to spend the day with us. He spent about three hours with Matt and me, and then the Management Board, testing us on every aspect of our plans, financial strategy, our faith decision process, and expansion plans. At the end of the day he sat me down and said he was so impressed by the unity of heart and the excellence in what we were doing that he would give us; wait for it, £50,000! I was speechless with joy as I knew today was the day we needed to pay the salary requests we had received. Praise God for his faithfulness right at the last moment. This together with the short-term interest free loans received during the day means we can pay a huge amount of the outstanding wages. I pray that my friend would somehow know what his generous spirit meant to me – what a guy!

I sent the following email to staff.

From: John Kirkby
Sent: 23 March 2006 13:45
To: All CAP Staff
Subject: Amazing miracle update

Hi CAP team

Latest miracles and precise situation as briefly as possible.

Headlines

£12,500 grant received yesterday added to £9,000 gift on Monday!! £50,000 gift from a businessman who we had been talking to regarding our needs!!! Other daily income: £1,700 today alone. Amazing response from staff!! £47,820 pledged, much already received. Two people lent £20, another donated £20. I am told by Janice that these were real and tremendous steps of faith for the staff members involved. One lent this from their rent money due next week. Praise God, we have been able to send this member of staff all they needed to meet their urgent bills. Also great emails from staff who literally have no money saying they would wait even longer if that helped other people. You know who you are and we are all amazed by your heart for others despite your own needs.

Outcome

Miracle of miracles, we actually managed to pay the entire request we had received for salaries needed by 25th!! These were paid just before 5pm last night, thirty minutes after we received the gift of £50,000. God has a real sense of timing and we are overwhelmed that we have been able to meet those pressing and urgent needs. Amazingly, we will also be paying all January outstanding salaries over the next few days and, providing the loans pledged are received, we have enough for the requests already received for salaries next week!! Please keep sending in your salary requests for what you need and when you need it and we will keep you informed as things develop.

So what next?

Please keep your offers of loans coming in, they are absolutely vital to ensuring we can meet the expected salary requests for April 1. For those who have pledged please get the cheques to us asap. It's very tight and days will make a difference.

We continue to do everything in our power to raise the money needed to get completely up to date for May 31. With all monies received and pledged we currently stand at approximately £200,000 still needed, this is down from £439,000 six weeks ago, that's £239,000 in six weeks!!!

I have been astonished by the emails I have received and the heart of support. All we can do is continue to believe God will finish this amazing journey he is taking us on and that, when he does, he will get all the glory.

John

I then read two emails that were in my inbox. It's so amazing that despite our ongoing difficulties every day lives are being changed through our centre network. This is what keeps us going.

From: CAP Centre Manager
Sent: 23 March 2006 12:23
To: John Kirkby
Subject: Recommitment to Christ

Praise God for this client. When I first met her she and her partner had just started going to church. Since then they have separated and she has been through all sorts of things, not least because most of their debts were in her name so she was left to repay them all herself. We've chatted along the way, but never actually sat down for a long talk. Last week she told me that she was renewing her confirmation vows, so I asked her about what had been happening to her in terms of her faith – and it was just so exciting!

She told me that she'd first come to know God as a teenager, and had a very strong faith but she then got married, divorced and fell out with the vicar when she wanted to have her daughter christened as a single mum. She left the church and moved away from God.

She felt she wanted to make some sort of public declaration of her faith and recommitment, and asked if she could renew the vows that she originally took as a teenager.

She's been through a lot since I took her on – she's been very strong and says that's because God has given her the strength to cope every step of the way.It was lovely seeing her in her church on Sunday – a precious moment!

CAP Centre Manager*

From: CAP Centre Manager
Sent: 23 March 2006 13:31
To: John Kirkby
Subject: New CAP baby

We have another CAP baby! She is new, but both her sister and mother are clients and were saved through CAP so she has been aware of our work and Jesus working in their lives. She wanted to read the 'Why Jesus?' booklet and pray on her own so I left her with it last week. She asked me for a Bible, so I took it up tonight. She told me she had prayed the prayer but didn't know if she had 'done it right' so she prayed again! I prayed for her to receive the Holy Spirit and left her sparkling! She had already told her boyfriend and is desperate to tell her Mum! Praise God!

CAP Centre Manager*

Tuesday April 4, 2006

I have just heard that our £730,000 bid to the government's financial inclusion fund has failed. Even though I'm not surprised it's still frustrating that the government just can't seem to see what incredible work we are doing here at CAP – really tackling poverty at a grassroots level. Many organisations will have been devastated upon hearing that their bids have been unsuccessful, but we will continue to press ahead with Plan A and expand.

Praise God that we are not dependent upon this kind of funding, and I thank him for the inspiration and perseverance to develop regular income from our 'Life Changer' programme. Some people still think we receive government funding – we don't! We need every pound that's donated – we can't do without it. As I've said before, please fill in a 'Life Changer' form at the back of the book – do it now!

Monday April 24, 2006

We need a good week this week as things are starting to tighten again. We still need £180,000 by 31 May and have wages due to be paid at the end of this week. New centre training starts Wednesday and we are getting ready for a very busy run up to our year end.

Tuesday April 25, 2006

£13,000 came in this morning!! One couple that have been so supportive over many years sent £8,000 in response to God's prompting. We also got another £5,000 from various small gifts. I pray that the people who send money, however small, will understand just how grateful we are for every penny they send. We simply could not do it without them.

Thursday April 27, 2006

We had a great night last night when the new centre managers came to our home for a meal and to spend some time with Lizzie and myself. Lizzie is always thrilled to meet the new centre managers and hear their different stories of how they came to CAP.

We also invited five members of staff from Bradford to share their stories including Debbie Thompson again, sharing how her life was before she came to CAP. To listen afresh to the suffering Debbie and her kids went through is truly humbling and really inspires us all to keep pressing forward for the hundreds of other Debbies out there that are literally dying because we can't get to them. I have been noticing in the papers just how many people have actually committed suicide due to debt. This has a profound effect on me. I list some below:

John, debts of £4,715: This 47-year-old salesman from Peterborough apparently committed suicide last week by taking painkillers, drinking whisky and walking into the sea. His father said, 'John had a mortgage for £99,000 yet the property was worth £180,000. He was four or five months behind, but the way the building society pursued him was inhumane.'

Paul, debts of £1,000: A 20-year-old student from Southampton, hanged himself last month. His mother said, 'He was worried by the letters that came from the bank. I'd forwarded them, but he never got around to opening them. He was a lovely and talented boy and we, his family, are utterly heartbroken.'

Michael, debts of £130,000: The 65-year-old mechanic from Reading gassed himself in his car in the family garage in January 2005. His widow said, 'It's wicked. Michael and the bank must have had contact with each other, they must have known how in debt he was. They should never have let this happen.'

David, debts of £65,000: *This week Elizabeth spent her second Valentine's Day without the man she loved. Her husband David, a 43-year-old technical writer and father of two, killed himself after amassing debts of £65,000. Grieving Elizabeth a 47 year old teaching assistant, says, 'David just wanted to be a good dad and provide for his family. He seemed to be so in charge of himself – he wasn't out drinking or spending loads of money on luxury items. But he liked to come home with flowers or buy me a cuddly toy if we were shopping. I just feel it's such a waste of a man everybody trusted.'*

Richard, debts of £100,000: *A 51-year-old forklift truck driver Richard hanged himself at his home in Loughborough in May 2004. His sister said, 'No one should be able to accumulate as many cards as Richard had. There should be tighter controls on credit allowed to individuals without equity to cover it.'*

Chris, debts of £70,000: *Chris, a 37-year-old engineer from Hull, hanged himself in July 2004. His widow said, 'I just couldn't believe a person could have that much debt.'*

Sarah, debts of £7,882: *The 26-year-old politics graduate from Milton Keynes hanged herself last July. Sarah's brother said, 'I simply don't understand how banks can sit back and watch someone getting into a helpless situation like this whilst all the time threatening legal action. I know she got a lot of letters and took the threats seriously. She believed she had to pay there and then.'*

Daniel, debts of £15,000: *Daniel, 21, a part-time worker from Bedford, hanged himself in August 2004. A family member said, 'It was the banks that put more than one nail in his coffin. Daniel had problems like any kid, but nothing* *that couldn't be sorted. When you're struggling you're not given a solution. You just get hounded with letters demanding payments.'*

(Names and towns all changed to protect identity.)

'He has sent me to bind up the brokenhearted.'

(Isaiah 61:1)

The truth is, if we could have got to them before they reached breaking point, I have no doubt we could have prevented their suicides. If we had centres in their areas they could have been alive today. It really is a life and death thing we are involved in and we can't hold back. We are literally saving lives, not just changing them.

Friday April 28, 2006

What a week! £31,000 in unexpected income and we have been able to pay all salary requests for the month end. We now need just £149,000 in the last four weeks to be up to date. I am overwhelmed by God's amazing provision and can't wait to see how he's going to do it.

Wednesday May 3, 2006

Great results for April – we have increased the number of clients we are helping by thirty-three per cent over the last year and the new centres we opened in October are really starting to do well. Over the last year we have seen 185 individuals make first time commitments to Christ as a direct result of our work – amazing!

Our seven new centre managers are back for week two of their initial training and they are doing so well. It's a real encouragement to the team here in Bradford to see the new centre managers. It brings home the reality of our growth and development and reminds us all that it's the centre managers we are here to serve. It's they who are on the front line and the whole church based centre network is the very cornerstone of our vision and plan to see this nation impacted through our work.

Tuesday May 9, 2006
4:15pm

What a couple of days we've just had! Monday was an amazing day with so much going on. We were filming for the new CAP DVD and two new centre managers are being interviewed for new centres due to open in September. It's so busy at the moment with loads of new stuff coming up.

We even had an assessment by the Centre for Social Justice who have short listed us for an award. They were so encouraged and inspired by how we have developed a charity that reaches the socially disadvantaged with a professional, twenty-first century answer. It's great to start being recognised for what God has done. Christians who are at the forefront of social change - that's where Jesus was and that's where we should be! (Stop press – at the awards ceremony in June we won!)

Monday May 15, 2006

Good day today. Matt and I went to give a presentation to the Business Awards panel. We have been short-listed in the 'customer focus' category. We went in front of a distinguished panel and both felt so relaxed. It's great for us when our efforts are acknowledged and is a real lift for the staff and supporters. We find out in July if we've won. (Stop press – we won again!)

We also had one of our best days for salvation with six individuals making first time commitments to Christ over the weekend. This means that today six people are starting a new life with God and the bell just kept ringing!

Tuesday May 23, 2006

With just eight days to go I have spent the morning working through our exact financial situation. It's amazing that over the last few days we have had quite a lot of money in, a thousand here, a few hundred there and some bills lower than expected. We find ourselves just £138,000 short which is quite amazing when you consider we needed over £437,000 in January!

I have decided I need to do something now. Although I know God can do some stuff last minute I have the responsibility to manage where I am in reality and we need to be up to date by next week.

Lizzie and I have been looking to see what we can do and have decided to remortgage our house and get about £36,000 from the equity. We see the house as God's anyway and providing CAP can repay us every month for three years we will be able to manage the increased mortgage payments. Matt and Josie also have the ability through their recent mortgage and house sale to lend some money in as well. This brings the total needed down to £94,000.

I also have one last phone call I can make to my friend who heads up the trust which previously agreed to give us £62,500 if we were able to match fund it by raising another three amounts of £62,500. He has already given us £12,500 so he might let us have the other £50,000. He was very open to help but just needed some time to consider.

Wednesday May 24, 2006

You will not believe what happened last night; even by our standards it was amazing. Firstly, I rang a supporter to say thank you for their support and she asked how we were doing. I explained we have great needs but were doing OK. At 9:00pm she rang me at home and told me they would send us £10,000 as a one-off gift plus lend us £25,000 interest free to be repaid whenever!! Also, my mate rang me back and confirmed the trust would release the £50,000. This means that we are only £9,000 short of being completely up-to-date. What an amazing turn around in just two days. Only God could be so intricate in making things work.

I also got the following email from Matt which is so encouraging about the actual results of all our efforts over the past few months. To be honest these are the result of amazing effort put in by all the staff over years and years.

From: Matt Barlow
Sent: 24 May 2006 16:08
To: All CAP Staff
Subject: Amazing achievements!

To all CAP staff

Well done! Well done! Well done! Well done everyone, but especially you centres!! Why?

Payouts
The total amount paid out by clients for bills and debts through their CAP account.

- For the first time ever payout is over half a million! It stormed up to £544,000 this month.
- Budget account payout for priority payments such as mortgage, rent, gas, electricity and council tax is up by 7.5% this month alone! Yes, you heard it right, one month's increase!
- This payout has increased by 44% over the last year!! That is half as much again as this time last year. Wow!
- The total paid by clients through their CAP account is up over the year by 67%!!! Well done centres and well done Creditor Liaison Unit. *(A department which*

negotiates with creditors to get payments agreed, interest and charges stopped.)

This means there are more people throughout the country who are now paying every bill on time and paying back their debt.

New Cases
- Average no. of cases over last 3 months = 96 per month (up from 70 for same period last year)

Salvations
- We have seen 183 first time decisions for Christ, up from 117 last year, an increase of 56%!!

Discipleship
- Discipleship figures – previously we saw 66% of all conversions moving on with their faith, we now see an incredible 84% of all conversions continuing with their faith - awesome!

God's hand of blessing is so clearly on us – to him goes all the glory as it is he that works through each of us to see his kingdom advance on a daily basis.

I am so proud of all we are achieving together.

Matt Barlow

Behind every one of these statistics are marriages staying together, homes not repossessed, families in control of their finances, debts being repaid, and people learning to save. Literally thousands of people are receiving life transforming work through a bunch of Christians simply dedicated to and motivated by God's heart for the poor.

Wednesday May 31, 2006
Well the day has arrived and I can't really believe it but it's all here – a combination of £5,500 in random gifts over the last week plus £1,000 from book sales and donations when I preached at Ealing Christian Centre on Sunday. The last amount came from clients.

We wrote to 1,900 clients asking if they would help with our coin trail (a fundraising event to raise a mile of coins). We sent them a card with space for ten £1 coins and have received just over £500 this morning! That's 50 clients saying we want to help.

What an amazing six months, and what an astonishing ten years. It's been such a privilege to see God's hand so evident in all we do. Can you believe it – he did it on the day!

We also had our best ever month for 'Life Changers.' Siân Wrangles, Donor Relations Manager, came in this afternoon to tell me we had 156 new 'Life Changers' this month!

It's so important for our ongoing development that we continue to see people support us with regular donations. If only people knew how important their £4 or £20 a month is to us. We are so grateful to everyone who gives in this way. If you haven't filled in a form then please do it now, they are printed at the end of the book. Don't wait until tomorrow – do it now! Please let the lasting testimony of this book be that you did what you could do!

Every time we receive a 'Life Changer' form which has come from readers of 'Nevertheless' we are so encouraged. You could always send us a cheque as well, because I'm sure that on whatever date you read this page there will be an unfolding miracle in our finances, and you a get chance to be featured in the next 'Nevertheless!'

Wednesday May 31, 2006

This afternoon we had a little party at work to celebrate our ten years. We all praised God for what he had done. We also anounced the final financial situation and everyone was so delighted that somehow we had managed to get through. I feel so proud of all the staff, for their individual faithfulness and amazing spirit they have shown over the years. I also found myself thinking about all the staff who had played a part over the years. I also thought of Paul Hubbard who was at my side for so many years, and continues to be very supportive and encouraging.

So what of the future? Well, it remains 'plan A.' We are really just at the beginning of an even more amazing story of what God has, is, and will continue to do through us. After ten years my overriding sense is still one of excitement at what lies ahead. I remain totally captivated by God's heart for the poor and his determination to reach the lost with his message of hope. I am thrilled to see the next generation coming through, and I am so delighted to see Matt take over as UK Chief Executive. I am excited about how God will continue to use me as I press forward with supporting the guys here in the UK and building the International Team.

What a privilege it has been to play my part in seeing this twenty-first century miracle unfold. To think of the thousands of people who woke up today with marriages intact that would have been over, in houses that would have been repossessed and with children that they couldn't afford to clothe and feed. Instead hundreds now have a personal relationship with God and are being discipled by the local church into the amazing future he has for them. It is truly breathtaking.

We have only just begun and I remain totally convinced that over the next ten years and the years after that, we will see Christians Against Poverty grow, touching and reaching hundreds of thousands of individual lives throughout the world with the love and grace of God.

The driving force behind all we do remains the same today as it was back in 1996. God's heart of love and compassion poured out for the poor and needy – to see his salvation break out and to see lives transformed through ordinary people based in local churches.

I hope you have been inspired and encouraged to do what you can do to advance the Kingdom of God.

To him be all the glory, honour and praise.

'Now to him who is able to do immeasurably more than all we ask or imagine, according to his power that is at work within us, to him be glory in the church and in Christ Jesus throughout all generations, for ever and ever! Amen.'

(Ephesians 3:20–21)

*All names and locations have been changed to protect anonimity

EPILOGUE

THE REAL REASON FOR CAP

As the book draws to a close, I wanted to end with the reason why we do what we do. The reason why we kept persevering through all the dark times, disappointments and challenges, the reason why we will continue to do all we can to expand the work of Christians Against Poverty is to change people's lives.

We have included just five stories out of the hundreds we have from the people we help. As you read these testimonies, I hope you will be encouraged and then inspired to become involved in Christians Against Poverty by doing what you can do to help other people see their lives transformed.

MAUREEN BREEN

'I got into trouble with the bank because of loans I took out to clear the debts that were left when my husband died and to help my daughter, as she has to manage with six children. I had to pay about £200 a month, but one payment got stolen and then I missed another month too so they were going to take me to court.

I knew I was in debt but I couldn't do anything about it; I couldn't think clearly. I started to get unwell as a result. I'm 70 years old and I couldn't move due to ulcers on my legs that developed after my husband died.

Maureen

In the end, my daughter went down to the Newport Advice Centre to see if they could help me and they put me in touch with Christians Against Poverty. Goff (Newport Centre Manager) and Yvonne (Support Worker) came to my house and took all the particulars down. They have lifted such a heavy weight of worry off my shoulders. They also introduced me to the church and I've made great friends.

I've always said my prayers, but it's different now, there is something inside now. I've found God and he has found me.

The girls from church clean my cupboards and do the hoovering for me. Other friends from church bring me flowers when they come every other Tuesday, and Angela brings me dinner on a Sunday. Without them I would be lonely, they've been absolutely wonderful. I feel enlightened; I've found God and all these lovely people.

In two or three years I'll be out of debt. I pray to God that he will help CAP. I thank God for CAP and for all the work they do.'

Maureen has since passed away but, praise God, we know she is in heaven. Through Maureen's story, her daughter also became a Christian.

CAROL & TONY JACKSON

'We had a few credit cards and a loan but my husband, Tony, had a well paid job so we could afford them. Then Tony got ill. He had blockages in his legs, then heart failure and then he lost a kidney. It was awful and he was laid off work. I had to reduce my hours to look after Tony because he was so ill.

Then the bills started coming but we just couldn't pay. I tried phoning the mortgage company to explain, but all they said was, "If you can't pay, we'll kick you out of your house." I knew we'd lose the house by Christmas. If we tried to talk about debt it would always turn into an argument. It was a complete nightmare, I felt as though I would burst under the pressure.

The worst thing is that people don't believe you're on the edge. You know you can't afford a loaf of bread, but people look at you like you're lying. Some weeks we couldn't even buy bread and milk. If I had no money for food we lived on tea and sugar to fill us up.

Then my sister told me about Christians Against Poverty so I phoned and told them the bailiffs were coming. When Tessa (Darlington Centre Manager) and Geraldine (Support Worker) came to my house I was so relieved. It felt as though a weight had been taken off us. It was like God had come to my door. I had put all my bills into six bin bags and when Tessa left with them I knew I had nothing to worry about. It was a lovely feeling knowing that no-one's going to knock at the door or phone me.

It's been fantastic working with CAP - they've got us back on track and we have enough money to eat properly. Every fortnight we put money into our CAP Account and they make sure our bills are paid for us. Because of our situation, bankruptcy was our best option. It took a year to save up the fees we needed and last Wednesday we went to court. It was so reassuring to have James (Support Worker) with us because I was so nervous.

Tony and Carol relax in their garden the week after their bankruptcy

When you are in debt you just think about bills all the time. Now I can think about getting my husband better. We are back to our old selves again and we talk to each other. We can laugh and have fun together instead of blaming each other for the situation we were in. Now I can honestly say that I love him again.

Over this time Tessa invited me to the Alpha course at her church, I said I'd give it a go but I didn't really like God much. I had given up on him as I'd had ten miscarriages and I thought I might lose my husband as well. One night a man talked about his life before and after he had become a Christian. I could really relate to his story and it made me want a change in my life. I can honestly say that God has given me the strength to keep going. It's a lovely feeling to know Jesus - I know he's there with me and it's wonderful.

After I had been going to church for two weeks Tony said I looked different, so he started going too. We went every week, and then we got baptised. We started going to home group every week because Tony said he didn't want to miss out. When Tony had his operation in January, they prayed and prayed. He could have died. My home group came round to be with me when he was in hospital, and took me to see him as I don't drive. It was a fantastic support. Everyone in church praying for him kept him alive.'

MAXINE THOMAS

'Life was stressful. I couldn't sleep because I was always thinking about how I would pay the creditors. One way I thought I could solve it was through having a lot of jobs. I had six jobs including a full time job. I was working my annual leave, weekends and evenings but all I was doing was paying off the interest on the debts, which were £30,000.

My standard of living wasn't good at all – I couldn't go out and the total amount of money I had for food was just £40 a month. I had to be very creative in how I spent my money and how I cooked. It came to the point where I decided enough was enough.

At the time, I was working in a hospital and I started going to the chapel there. I found a copy of 'Word for Today' – at the back it had a salvation prayer and I gave my life to God. I poured out my heart and soul into a letter and sent it off to the address at the back of the book.

Three months later I got a phone call from a pastor called Sheila. She invited me to church and counselled me. I told her about my debts and she gave me some information about Christians Against Poverty.

Maxine

At that point, I was so relieved because I knew I would get help and support – the burden just lifted. From then on I just redirected any letters to CAP and that took away the stress totally.

As a consequence of becoming a CAP client, I now offer support to other people who are in debt. I have learnt how to budget and my standard of living has improved – I can now socialise, which I couldn't do before. Since becoming a Christian, the fellowship with people at church is now crucial to me, as they offer so much support. When you're going through debt, you withdraw and you don't socialise because of the lack of money, but once the stress has been taken away, you are able to talk and testify how good God is and how 'stressless' you are now!'

BOBBY MUNN

'Before I met Dan I was in trouble – I was £700 in debt. This may not sound like a lot to some people, but when you don't have access to a bank account and you can't make your finances balance, it's a big problem. I got into debt when I was ripped off by two men who lived in the flat below me. They abused my trust by racking up long distance calls on my phone and stealing my savings. I had to keep the money at home because I couldn't access a bank account. I borrowed money from friends and family to tide me over. I spoke to the housing manager about my situation and they moved me to Wandsworth. The move cost me money too.

I didn't know what to do about my financial situation. It was really stressing me out, everyone wanted money. All my plans were shattered by not having money. I was barely living on benefits. I was really miserable.

A friend of mine suggested I ring Christians Against Poverty. Dan (Wandsworth Centre Manager) came to see me right away. He took all my bills to sort out a budget for me. I didn't have a cooker or flooring so Dan helped me get them through another organisation. I felt great with Dan helping me. I felt like people loved me because they did all this for free. Without CAP I would have drowned. I felt like a ship that had been stuck in a storm but which survived. It couldn't sail due to a broken mast, and my heart was the mast. My mind was lost too, the dreadful tides carried it every which way.

I've been working with CAP now for two years. It's been so much easier since Dan came along. It was so helpful to have a budget broken down for me showing how much I have coming in, and where it all needs to go. Dan made it so easy to understand, I know how much I need, how much I have, and now I can save! I know I just have to pay into my CAP account regularly and everyone gets paid that needs to be paid.

*Bobby (left) with Clive Boldy at the Discovery Break
where he became a Christian!*

I never really thought about becoming a Christian until I was invited on CAP's Discovery Break. Susan from CAP rang and asked me if I wanted to go on a three-day break away to the north of England. I was a bit sceptical but then she mentioned horse riding. I love that and I was very keen to go then. We went on an open top bus – what a great time. We played chess and I just felt so much at home! The meals were amazing and out of this world. We also did some square dancing as a group, which was a good laugh. Everyone was just so amazing and so full of love and joy; there was so much laughter. It was great.

There were also opportunities to sit around and chat. I spoke to Mike (a CAP client who became a Christian and has done volunteer work for CAP). He asked me if I was a Christian and I said no. He issued me a challenge to become a Christian saying that it was a really important decision. One night Penny (Dunfermline Centre Manager) came and spoke to me too. She asked me what my excuse was for not becoming a Christian. I told her that I wasn't good enough. She said it wasn't a good enough excuse and that God loved everyone, no matter what they'd done, or who they were. So I prayed the prayer and asked God into my life. Susan was thrilled and Mike was stunned. He said it was about time. I had a brilliant time on the Discovery Break, it changed my life.

CAP's made such a tremendous difference in my life. I've now got goals to aim for. I can now plan and save for things. God knows I love him, and he's there for me. It's really cool.'

PETER AND NICOLE WRIGHT

'I [Peter] wanted to tell you my story because, without people like you, things would have been very different for me and my family. The Fleetwood Centre had only been open three months when I phoned and I can't imagine where I'd be now if Christians Against Poverty hadn't been there. We wouldn't have a house, I'd still be failing my family and I'd be absolutely desperate.

In April 1995 my left foot was amputated following an accident at work. A few years later I took out a loan but following a review my Disability Living Allowance was stopped and I was stuck with a debt I couldn't pay. I set up my own business as a mechanic but a year down the line I suffered a mild stroke that left me unable to work. Nicole was being exploited by an employer paying less than the minimum wage. It got to the point where we couldn't afford the shopping so we'd miss paying a bill so that we could afford to live. We used to go without the gas so that we could afford the electric, but that meant warming up kettles of water to bath the kids. We couldn't afford anything.

Then the difficulties started with our marriage. I was constantly worrying about the long hours Nicole was working, but she would say that it needed to be done to pay the bills and put food on the table. It felt like Nicole had all the pressure on her and I felt a bit useless because I had not long had my stroke. I was struggling even to look after the children while Nicole was out trying to earn enough money to live. We were just biting each other's heads off all the time. Debt also had an affect on the children. We were very agitated and tired and we seemed to shout at them for every little thing. I felt like I'd let the kids down because I couldn't provide for them.

We stopped opening the letters because we knew what they all said. I felt better ignoring the situation because it wasn't getting any better when I was trying to deal with it. We were just getting further and further into debt. The last letter that came through the door was a repossession order two weeks before Christmas. It got to the point that we thought if they take the house they'll have taken everything, so we'll have nothing else to lose. We just felt that life wasn't worth living anymore.

Before phoning CAP we tried a couple of solicitors. One told us they were sorry but we'd gone too far down the line and the house was as good as gone. That was the same day that we saw the advert for CAP in the paper. We weren't going to bother but then we thought, it's our last hope, it's got to be worth a try – so I rang CAP.

Dave (Fleetwood Centre Manager) had to tell us that he didn't know if we could save the house or not, but he was willing to try. At least someone was here to help us. We had to look at council housing as an option and all that was on offer was a one-bedroom flat with no cooking facilities. We had an emergency court hearing the next day one hour before we were due to be evicted, and fortunately Dave got the case adjourned – it meant that we had a house over Christmas and that was a success in itself.

After Dave's first visit, he kept us in the know as much as he could. Some days he would even ring us to see how we were and it was nice to be treated as an individual and not just another customer. The second time we went to court, it was my daughter's birthday. We were singing 'Happy Birthday' to her, trying to keep things normal for the kids but we knew that an hour later we'd be stood in court and could face losing the house. We couldn't buy her anything for her birthday but all we hoped for was that she'd have a house to come home to.

The day I found out we could keep the house was amazing. It was like heaven, like having a fresh start. Dave sorted out a budget and we actually had a set amount to live off for shopping, which was great. After about four or five weeks, we could see that the bills were being paid and we started to see the benefits. We could buy the kids the odd little thing at a weekend and we could actually buy a week's shopping and not just have to buy a loaf of bread. We knew it was going to work.

The future looks fantastic now. We can see a life ahead of us and a life for our children. We started going to church through CAP because Dave used to pray with us before going to court and I thought, "Oh well, it's working, so what's there to lose really?" We had seen the benefits of praying and believing, so we started on an Alpha course that Dave invited us to. I became a Christian on January 18, 2006 and after a few sessions Nicole asked God into her life too.

Being a Christian is the best move I've ever made. I thought that believing in God was enough. He's in our lives in a big way now. I realised that Jesus had been with us all the way through – he had been to court with us and had helped us out. He works closely with us and I thank him for coming into our lives the way he has done and for helping us through. I am soon going to be training to be part of Dave's

Peter and Nicole with their daughters and Dave Tudor (left)

Support Team. I want to be able to help anyone who's going through what we've been through.

We now give a monthly donation to CAP of £6.50 and I want to ask if you would give, even £2 or £3 a month, it would really help. There are thousands of people out there going through what we've been through and we need to see CAP grow bigger so that more people can be helped out in the same way. I wanted to tell my story to help you see how bad it can get for someone in debt and how important it is that you give to CAP. It needs to be given, if there is any way you can give it, just do it. It will save more lives.'

'Life Changer' forms are at the back of this book. Please help us help more people like Maureen, Carol and Tony, Maxine, Bobby and Peter and Nicole. Please become a 'Life Changer' today – we need your support!

MY FAMILY

I am often asked how we have survived in the midst of all that has happened. My answer is that we are very well! We obviously had some very difficult times, particularly during the first three to four years when we gave up our home and moved into rented accommodation with Lizzie seven months pregnant. As you know I had two great daughters, Jasmine and Jessica, from my first marriage. On April 13, 1999 Lizzie gave birth to our beautiful first child together, Abigail.

Abigail is a real character, full of drive and I would say she is a born leader. She is very bright and has an amazing capacity to absorb information. She is razor sharp and can be very determined, which can occasionally lead to some heated moments. She is a wonderful challenge and it wouldn't surprise me if she changes the world given the right opportunity.

In November 2000 we had a real miracle in our own lives when we managed to buy our own home. That house was a real blessing to us. We decorated the whole house and installed a new kitchen in four weeks and moved in just before Christmas 2000.

May 2001 saw the birth of Thomas. What a joy after three wonderful girls to get a boy. Tom is a gorgeous kid, full of beans and already eating us out of house and home! He is naturally compassionate and kind to others. It's great to see our formerly 'girly' house with a few spiders, sharks, dinosaurs and fire engines thrown in. Who says stereotyping is dead!

We really enjoyed the sense of God's amazing blessing for us as a family and to a certain extent we simply settled down. Lizzie had her hands full with the little ones and naturally her practical involvement in CAP's work became less. However, her contribution to CAP by releasing and supporting me was never in doubt and came at some personal cost to her.

Then, on February 24, 2004, our beautiful daughter Lydia Joy was born. She is such a joy, full of life and well able to hold her own in a somewhat hectic household. She is so loved by all her siblings and adds so much to our family.

My children are a great blessing to me and it has been such a joy to see how my older girls and the little ones have merged together into one big family. There are a lot of us about when we're all together and it gets quite noisy but it's always great fun! (Well perhaps not always!)

Jasmine finished her three-year degree course in Psychology at Bangor University in July 2008, graduating with a first! In August 2008 she married her long-term boyfriend Simon. Jaz has also joined CAP as part of the Partnership Team. Can you believe that my gorgeous first-born daughter, who went through so much all those years ago is now so strong in herself and in her faith. I am so delighted that I will get to work alongside her for many years to come. Having worked and volunteered for CAP over her teenage years she well and truly deserves this job, and she brings so much to the team.

Jessica has gone to university to study midwifery. She did amazingly well to even get an offer, as there were over seven hundred applicants for just twenty-two places and she passed her first year with flying colours. My little baby has grown up! We love her dearly and miss her vibrancy when she's away. She is so full of life and I am delighted that she has come through everything so strong and is such a great friend. She is relaxed, warm, friendly, and keeps me on my toes in one way or another. I am delighted to see Jess pursue her dream of becoming a

John and Lizzie with (from left) Jasmine, Lydia,
Tom, Abigail, Simon and Jessica

midwife. If you are planning on having a baby sometime around 2011 and onwards in the Bradford area, look out for Jess!

It's so amazing to see God work through all the difficult times we had back in the early nineties. My relationship and friendship with the girls is one of God's great blessings in my life. I look forward to watching all my children grow in their understanding of God's love for them, and to serve him in whatever role he has for their lives.

Over 2008 I had the privilege of being part of a church plant in the centre of Bradford. The Light Church, as it is called, is incredible. It has been wonderful to watch the church grow and really develop such a heart for the local community. Our vision is 'loving God and loving people' and we are committed to reaching out to the lost through our church. I am on the leadership team and it has been great to see the church from a leader's perspective. It really makes me appreciate the challenges and conflicting demands that the local church has and I look forward to seeing how the church grows and develops over the coming months and years.

What about our life from a financial point of view? God has outrageously blessed this particular part of our lives. We moved to a beautiful new home in October 2005 and each morning when I wake up I can't quite get over how amazing both the house and garden are. Lizzie and I often say to each other, 'Whose house is this? Do we actually live here?' God has completely repaid the financial sacrifice we made during the early years of CAP. We continue to hold all God's gifts to us very lightly with a continued sense of awe that he could transform our lives and be so faithful to us.

Lizzie remains completely committed to the heart of CAP and is so supportive in all I do. She is gracious, kind, loving and full of encouragement, holding it all together to provide a great home environment for us all. With three young children, her job at Bradford Christian School and keeping tabs on me, her life is very full!

With my growing international role, we spent four months from January to April 2008 in Australia working with CAP and also pioneering the work in New Zealand. We had an amazing time together and had our faith stretched, tested and saw God achieve so much. The kids enjoyed the whole experience immensely and settled into Aussie life like they were born for it. It was also a great blessing for Lizzie to work alongside the Australia team and for us to see so many lives being changed at the other side of the world. We serve an awesome God!

Although our sacrifice as a couple is different from the early days, it remains small in comparison with the joy we both feel at seeing God use our lives for so much good in the midst of such outrageous personal blessings from him.

As a family we would like to thank everyone who has helped us, stood with us and supported our life in any way over the years. We are blessed with such great friends, wonderful children, and a great ministry and future. God is so good and has done so much. We just sense the blessings are not over and look forward to God continuing to grow and prosper our life both as a couple and as a family.

CAP INTERNATIONAL

You will have read a little about the beginnings of CAP's international work in chapter nine. However, I'm sure it will be no surprise to learn that it did not stop there! CAP has already spread to New Zealand and we have plans to pioneer this fantastic ministry in other countries as well. I thought it would be great to let the key members of our Australian and New Zealand teams explain more about the journey of CAP in these two countries.

CAP Australia: Ross and Alison's Story

'In 2003, Alison and I felt God call us to the United Kingdom. We were well aware that this meant leaving behind our family, friends and life as we knew it, but we were up for the challenge. We knew little at the time of where God was taking us and of the plans he had prepared, but we had a strong conviction that he wanted us to take this step of faith.

With this in mind we both resigned from well paid jobs and relocated to Bradford, West Yorkshire with our children Kealy and Curtis. With no jobs, no schools, no home and no car, we quickly came to rely on God for all our needs. Little did we know at the time that this was the beginning of a faith journey like no other.

Ali and I had previously been familiar with the work of CAP as our church had opened the first CAP Centre in Australia. As "Life Changers," we had been introduced to John, so when we arrived in the UK it seemed like getting in contact with him was a natural thing to do.

When I phoned John for some advice on "life in the UK," I was overwhelmed by his incredible generosity and openness towards me and my family. Not only did he give great advice, but he and his wife Lizzie opened up their home for a week as we found our feet in a new country. We will never forget the warmth we received when they flung open the front door and stood with arms wide open. We immediately felt like long lost friends!

It didn't take long for our conversation to turn towards CAP and John mentioned there happened to be jobs available in various departments. With a real sense of excitement, we both felt that this was the right thing to do and sent our applications in. We started work a few weeks later and haven't looked back since.

Our time in the UK was one of incredible growth, developing faith and stirring up our passion to reach a hurting world with the love of Christ. In the years that have followed we have continued to be amazed by God's faithfulness to us, as we spend ourselves on behalf of the poor and needy - not only in the UK, but here in Australia.

Since returning to Australia in January 2007 and joining the management team, we have been continually amazed at God's miraculous provision. As we boldly step out in faith and reach people in financial crisis, God continues to provide for the ministry in ways that we never thought possible.

In the last twelve months alone, hundreds of clients have begun the journey towards financial freedom and dozens of families have become debt free. Our greatest joy though is for the many clients who have made first time decisions for Christ and are now connected to a local church.

The long-term vision for CAP Oz is to have over 200 CAP centres throughout Australia! We know there will be many challenges along the way, but the price is well worth paying for the thousands of lives that are going to be impacted in the years to come through the work of Christians Against Poverty.

We count it an absolute joy and privilege to play our part in CAP Australia and in seeing our nation transformed.'

Ross Buttenshaw
National Director for CAP Australia

They have many of the same struggles we face, yet they have shown the same resilience and determination to get the job done. They are great people committed wholeheartedly to God's vision for CAP. We will use all we have learned as we now see the expansion of our international work over the coming years.

'CAP Oz' was the first, and proved we could do great things with God and a few brave people willing to go for it.

CAP New Zealand: Heather and Gareth's Story

'We arrived in New Zealand on November 1, 2007 with just enough money to cover our expenses for the first two months. We also needed to find somewhere to live, some offices, a car and supporters who would grab hold of the vision.

Within the first week, we managed to find a home at a fantastic price, fully furnished (which is almost unheard of in Auckland), with a spare room where we could have our office. After having borrowed two different cars from generous people for the first few weeks we then managed to buy a car recommended to us by a great mechanic. Right from the beginning God was looking after us and things were slotting into place.

John's first visit was in November 2007. It was just an amazing week of meetings with the most well connected people, and interviews on the main Christian radio station and TV channel! To top it all off, we had about twenty people say they would become "Life Changers," and a fantastic couple that were so moved by John's story and CAP UK's client testimonies that they gave us $10,000 to see us through the

John with the CAP NZ team

next two months! There are just endless stories, even in these first few months, of God's amazing provision for us.

Before Christmas we saw our first two clients. We wanted to prove, before we started opening centres, that the debt counselling was going to work in New Zealand, and it did! Our clients paid into their CAP Account within a couple of weeks of us seeing them and they are now on their way to a debt free future!

December also saw our first two CAP centres, Alive Church in Whangarei and Blockhouse Bay Baptist in Auckland, take a step of faith and sign up with us. Our first two CAP NZ centres!

The Centre Managers were trained in February and started seeing clients mid-March. After just four weeks, it was so obvious that there is such a huge need here in NZ. We had 25 clients booked in for visits by the end of the first month! The most fantastic news is that we also had our first salvation! It is amazing, not only to see God changing lives through finances, but changing lives for eternity as well. Since those early days CAP NZ has simply gone from strength to strength. I have been so impressed with the commitment of our staff. The faith they have shown in God and the work of CAP NZ has truly humbled me. They have joined us despite the fact that we are new and have yet to prove ourselves. These people are truly an incredible testimony.

In our first eighteen months, we opened five centres and offered hope and a solution to 556 people. These included people who, until then, had not been able to feed or clothe themselves properly, single mums who simply could not make it on their own and so many who were living in fear and depression because of their finances. We saw 38 people become Christians during this time. These statistics really show how CAP is transforming lives.

God has truly blessed CAP in New Zealand. The country was ready and is so open to CAP, churches are desperate to set up centres in their communities. We feel very blessed to have had the privilege of coming to the other side of the world to expand this amazing charity and have really seen God's hand all over it.

We want this success to continue. CAP NZ's vision is to have 175 centres in every town and suburb in New Zealand within ten years! Even though we are on the other side of the world, God is still the same! He has been so faithful to us, and we are confident that he will continue to bless this ministry just as he has in the UK and in Australia. We have the same heart and the same vision as CAP UK and CAP Oz, which is to see the nation of New Zealand changed one life at a time as we release people from the burden of debt and show them something of Christ's love. Praise God for his love, grace and faithfulness!'

Heather & Gareth Jones
CAP NZ

Heather and Gareth are a truly remarkable couple! Heather has worked with us for five years, doing amazing work with HOPE (our IT case management system), and managing the Central Payments Unit. I was sad for CAP UK, but delighted for New Zealand when Heather came and told us that she believed God was calling them to pioneer CAP there. As a couple they are so capable and I have had the real privilege of working closely with them to launch the charity in a completely new country. It has certainly been an incredible journey so far – taking me right back to my pioneering roots!

Over the last few years I have been conscious of the fact that God may have a bigger vision than us for where CAP may end up. We have a unique, world-class and state-of-the-art debt counselling service that works with local churches providing them with a tool that reaches into their local communities to effectively tackle poverty. We also now have a brilliant financial education course, CAP Money, which further equips churches for community outreach. I have begun to see that God is starting to create opportunities for CAP and, in particular, CAP Money to expand into other countries. An example of this is the 2009 piloting of CAP Money in Norway, where it has had a great reception.

Our international work certainly has long-term strategy, but the only way to make CAP work is by being committed to the long haul and establishing an organisation capable of taking on such a huge social problem. We have also set up an International Operations Team to oversee the whole global development of CAP.

I am excited about the future of the charity's international work and, as always, I remain overwhelmed that God would give me the privilege of continuing to serve him all over the world. Who would have thought when I first started twelve years ago, with a ten pound note from a small home office, that we would now have an International Board working both here in the UK, Australia and now New Zealand! It is amazing and somewhat overwhelming!

2010 UPDATE

As I sit here fourteen years after setting out on the journey of CAP I simply can't believe just what has been achieved. We now have over 110 centres nationwide and are helping more than 13,000 people every year – isn't God good! In addition we have distributed approximately 80,000 copies of Nevertheless! I never thought when I started my diary back in 1996 that so many people would find my story such an inspiration and challenge to them.

It is my delight to tell you that 2009 was a great year for CAP financially. We saw huge growth in our regular income from individuals and finished 2009 with every salary paid up-to-date in all three countries. As you can imagine, this is a miracle! Our needs for 2010 and beyond remain in the realm of faith, meaning that the area in which we need to see the biggest growth is our 'Life Changer' regular giving scheme.

Things continue to develop internationally for CAP too. You will have read from Ross Buttenshaw that CAP Australia has continued to go from strength to strength. The team out there have been amazing. There have been trials and difficulties over the last twelve months, but they have faced them all with a spirit of determination and faith that has often left me humbled. By the end of the year, there will be 25 CAP centres in Australia. They have come such a long way and I am so proud of the team. They are impacting Australia in the most incredible way.

CAP New Zealand has now been running for two and a half years. It is amazing to think what they have achieved in such a short time. Heather and Gareth truly did an incredible job and God has really blessed the whole operation. We now have six centres and will have doubled the centre network by the end of 2010. We have also sent out two great members of our UK staff, Simon Wilce and Tara Kirby. It is such an encouragement to see these young people so full of vision and purpose and so willing to leave their friends and family to fly halfway across the world and help the poor and needy.

So what of the UK? Apart from coming top of the Sunday Times' 'Best 100 Small Companies to Work For' list for the second year running, we have developed and launched CAP Money, which I mentioned briefly in the last chapter. I first ran this course at my local church several years ago and people were blown away by it. The overwhelmingly positive feedback I received really inspired us to develop CAP Money across the UK for every church to use in a similar way to the Alpha Course. The course consists of three short DVD presentations followed by practical budgeting help for individuals led

John with Matt Barlow and members of the CAP Money Team.

by CAP Money Coaches. CAP Money Coaches are volunteers from the
CAP Money church who have been specially trained by CAP.

This is one of the biggest initiatives we have ever undertaken
and its success has surpassed even our outrageous expectations.
Since we launched it in January 2008 we have 500 churches across the
UK running CAP Money Courses with 1500 trained Money Coaches
and around 10,000 people have attended a CAP Money Course at the
time of printing this book. Lives are being transformed as people have
found a radical yet simple way to manage their finances. How good
is our God! If you would like more information about CAP Money
please visit www.capmoney.org.

In terms of our Centre Network, the future looks very exciting. As
I mentioned at the start we now have over 110 centres with over 150
staff members here in Bradford and 250 volunteers, centre managers
and debt coaches across the rest of the UK. However, we are not
content to sit back and just celebrate that achievement. There are still
people across the UK who need our help. We have therefore decided
to open 80 more centres in 2010. This will mean that, in 2010 alone,
we will help 6,000 new families! We have the infrastructure, the faith
and the drive as well as world-class people to achieve this outrageous
challenge. This is certainly a giant step forward in our vision to see this
nation changed one life at a time. Above all else, the fact that since this
ministry began, we've seen over 2000 individuals come to know Christ
worldwide is awe inspiring! Across the three CAP countries, we are
seeing an average of 50 people becoming Christians every month and
yes, we do still ring the bell at head office and pray for every one of
them – it's a huge privilige to be able to do this.

People often ask me how I feel with such massive growth and
responsibility. The answer; I feel exactly the same as in 1996 when I
sat in my bedroom looking out over Bradford and feeling God's love
and heart for the poor of that city. My faith in God is still as strong as
ever, and I am confident that he will continue to pour out his blessing
over the work.

Once again, Isaiah 58 comes to mind.

> *'If you do away with the yoke of oppression, with the pointing*
> *finger and malicious talk, and if you spend yourselves on behalf*
> *of the hungry and satisfy the needs of the oppressed, then your*
> *light will rise in the darkness, and your night will become like*
> *the noonday. The Lord will guide you always; he will satisfy your*
> *needs in a sun-scorched land and will strengthen your frame.*
> *You will be like a well-watered garden, like a spring whose waters*
> *never fail.'*
>
> *(Isaiah 58:9-11)*

His word says 'if.' As an organisation and personally, we have made the decision to spend ourselves whatever the cost to see our work continue. We know that we really do meet the genuine needs of the oppressed in this twenty-first century society, therefore we can stand on the promises that follow.

He will guide us and satisfy our needs in a sun-scorched land. We will be like a well-watered garden. These are the same promises I have seen over and over again for the last fourteen years.

We are confident that God will continue to guide and strengthen us as individuals and as an organisation. By growing us as individuals, and with thousands more journeying with us we grow stronger. We will see continuous miraculous provision in a sometimes sun-scorched land. CAP is certainly a well-watered garden, full of fruit. For me, I remain certain that CAP will continue to grow in fruitfulness as marriages are held together, children are fed, homes are not repossessed and people are saved. That's the fruit of our future, as we continue year upon year as we expand across the UK and internationally. Isaiah says,

> *'Your people will rebuild the ancient ruins and will raise up the*
> *age-old foundations; you will be called Repairer of Broken Walls,*
> *Restorer of Streets with Dwellings.'*
>
> *(Isaiah 58:12)*

Together with partner churches, and the tens of thousands of people who support CAP, we will continue to raise up the age-old foundations of the church by being relevant to the society in which we have been born, meeting needs and bringing hope to thousands.

In the same way that people like Wilberforce, who abolished slavery, and the Booths, founders of the Salvation Army, rose up in their generation to see society changed, I am confident that in the next few years CAP will change the very society in which we find ourselves.

I pray that you are inspired to do all you can do to see this miracle of God grow and flourish. As I conclude this latest instalment in what God has achieved from one broken man in a bedroom with a tenner, to a world-changing ministry, I am again reminded that it's God who deserves the glory, honour and praise.

John Kirkby
January 2010

PLAY YOUR PART:
BECOME A LIFE CHANGER

CAP receives no government funding for its work and so we rely on the generosity of individuals and churches who share our passion to bring justice and salvation to those suffering in debt and poverty. People like you!

At CAP we believe we are living in a miracle. People give what they can, and somehow God provides for us and therefore the thousands of people we are helping. It's just like the miracle of the loaves and fish. Please join us in this miracle by becoming a Life Changer and making a regular donation. Just fill in the form opposite or call 01274 760761. Join us and make our vision a reality; let's change this nation together.

Become a **LIFE CHANGER**

CHRISTIANS AGAINST POVERTY **UK**

Changing lives. One life at a time.

YOUR DETAILS – PLEASE COMPLETE IN BLOCK CAPITALS

Title: Forename:

Surname:

First line of address:

      Postcode:

Tel: Mobile:

Email:

Where did you get this form?

YOUR GIFT:

I/We would like to make a monthly gift of £3   £5   £10   £20   £50   or £.......
on the   **1st   8th   15th   28th   (please select)** of each month until further notice.
The first payment will be made in .... (please state month)

GIFT AID DECLARATION:

☐ I am **not** a UK taxpayer.   ☐ I don't know what this means – please call me to explain.

☐ I am a UK taxpayer and I would like Christians Against Poverty to reclaim tax on all my donations as from 1 April 07.*

Signature: ....   Date: _ _ / _ _ / _ _

You must pay income tax and/or capital gains tax at least equal to the amount we claim on your donation in the tax year (currently 28p for every £1 that you give). Please notify Christians Against Poverty if you change your name and/or address. Reg. Charity N° 1097217.

CHRISTIANS AGAINST POVERTY **UK**

Instruction to your Bank/Building Society to pay by Direct Debit

DIRECT Debit

Originators Identification N°: 8 3 7 3 8 5

Please return to: Supporter Relations Team, CAP, Jubilee Mill, North Street, Bradford, BD1 4EW (registered office)

Name and full postal address of your Bank/Building Society

To: The Manager: Address:
Bank/Building Society:
....

Instruction to your Bank/Building Society
Please pay Christians Against Poverty Direct Debits from the account detailed in this instruction, subject to the safeguards assured by the Direct Debit Guarantee. I understand that this instruction may remain with Christians Against Poverty and if so details will be passed electronically to my bank/building society.

Name(s) of account holder(s) ....
Branch Sort Code   Bank/building society account number   Date: _ _ / _ _ / _ _

☐☐ ☐☐ ☐☐   ☐☐☐☐☐☐☐☐   Signature: ....

Banks and Building Societies may not accept Direct Debit instructions for some types of account

Registered charity No. 1097217 Charity Registered in Scotland No. SC038776 Company Limited by Guarantee, Registered in England and Wales No. 4655171

The Direct Debit Guarantee: The Direct Debit Guarantee should be detached and retained by the payer. **DIRECT Debit**

This guarantee is offered by all Banks and Building Societies that take part in the Direct Debit scheme. The efficiency and security of the scheme is monitored and protected by your own Bank or Building Society. If the amounts to be paid or the payment dates change, Christians Against Poverty will notify you 10 working days in advance of your account being debited or as otherwise agreed. If an error is made by Christians Against Poverty or your Bank or Building Society, you are guaranteed a full and immediate refund from your branch of the amount paid. You can cancel a Direct Debit at any time by writing to your Bank or Building Society. Please also send a copy of your letter to us.

PLAY YOUR PART:
BECOME A LIFE CHANGER

CAP receives no government funding for its work and so we rely on the generosity of individuals and churches who share our passion to bring justice and salvation to those suffering in debt and poverty. People like you!

At CAP we believe we are living in a miracle. People give what they can, and somehow God provides for us and therefore the thousands of people we are helping. It's just like the miracle of the loaves and fish. Please join us in this miracle by becoming a Life Changer and making a regular donation. Just fill in the form opposite or call 01274 760761. Join us and make our vision a reality; let's change this nation together.

Become a  LIFE CHANGER

CHRISTIANS
AGAINST POVERTY UK

Changing lives. One life at a time.

YOUR DETAILS – PLEASE COMPLETE IN BLOCK CAPITALS

Title: [ ][ ][ ] Forename: [ ][ ][ ][ ][ ][ ][ ][ ][ ][ ][ ][ ][ ][ ][ ]

Surname: [ ][ ][ ][ ][ ][ ][ ][ ][ ][ ][ ][ ][ ][ ][ ][ ][ ][ ]

First line of address: [ ][ ][ ][ ][ ][ ][ ][ ][ ][ ][ ][ ][ ][ ][ ][ ]

[ ][ ][ ][ ][ ][ ][ ][ ][ ][ ][ ][ ] Postcode: [ ][ ][ ][ ][ ][ ]

Tel: [ ][ ][ ][ ][ ][ ][ ][ ] Mobile: [ ][ ][ ][ ][ ][ ][ ][ ]

Email: [ ][ ][ ][ ][ ][ ][ ][ ][ ][ ][ ][ ][ ][ ][ ][ ][ ][ ]

Where did you get this form? [   ]

YOUR GIFT:

I/We would like to make a monthly gift of £3   £5   £10   £20   £50   or £.......
on the   **1st   8th   15th   28th   (please select)** of each month until further notice.
The first payment will be made in .... (please state month)

GIFT AID DECLARATION:

[ ] I am **not** a UK taxpayer.   [ ] I don't know what this means – please call me to explain.

[ ] I am a UK taxpayer and I would like Christians Against Poverty to reclaim tax on all my donations as from 1 April 07.

Signature: ....   Date: _ _ / _ _ / _ _
You must pay income tax and/or capital gains tax at least equal to the amount we claim on your donation in the tax year (currently 28p
or every £1 that you give). Please notify Christians Against Poverty if you change your name and/or address. Reg. Charity Nº 1097217.

CHRISTIANS
AGAINST POVERTY UK

**Instruction to your Bank/Building Society
to pay by Direct Debit**

DIRECT Debit

Originators Identification Nº: [8][3][7][3][8][5]

Please return to: Supporter Relations Team, CAP, Jubilee Mill, North Street, Bradford, BD1 4EW (registered office)

Name and full postal address of your Bank/Building Society

To: The Manager: Address:
Bank/Building Society:
....

Instruction to your Bank/Building Society
Please pay Christians Against Poverty Direct Debits from the account detailed in this instruction, subject to the
safeguards assured by the Direct Debit Guarantee. I understand that this instruction may remain with Christians
Against Poverty and if so details will be passed electronically to my bank/building society.

Name(s) of account holder(s) ....

Branch Sort Code   Bank/building society account number   Date: _ _ / _ _ / _ _

[ ][ ][ ] [ ][ ][ ]   [ ][ ][ ][ ][ ][ ][ ][ ]   Signature: ....

Banks and Building Societies may not accept Direct Debit instructions for some types of account

Registered charity No. 1097217 Charity Registered in Scotland No. SC038776 Company Limited by Guarantee, Registered in England and Wales No. 46551

The Direct Debit Guarantee: The Direct Debit Guarantee should be detached and retained by the payer.

DIRECT Debit

This guarantee is offered by all Banks and Building Societies that take part in the Direct Debit scheme. The efficiency and security of the scheme
is monitored and protected by your own Bank or Building Society. If the amounts to be paid or the payment dates change, Christians Against
Poverty will notify you 10 working days in advance of your account being debited or as otherwise agreed. If an error is made by Christian
Against Poverty or your Bank or Building Society, you are guaranteed a full and immediate refund from your branch of the amount paid. You can
cancel a Direct Debit at any time by writing to your Bank or Building Society. Please also send a copy of your letter to us.

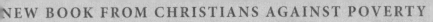

JOURNEYS OF HOPE

SPECIAL READER OFFER...

£3.99

We're offering you the opportunity to purchase CAP's newest book, Journeys of Hope, at the fantastic discount price of just £3.99 (RRP £5.99).

We hope you'll be encouraged and inspired as you read twelve stories of people whose paths have crossed with Christians Against Poverty. You will be amazed as you read of God's transforming power at work in their lives.

Order your copy by filling in a form from the back of this book.

ORDER YOUR COPY NOW!

JOURNEYS OF HOPE

12 LIVES CHANGED BY **GOD**
CHRISTIANS AGAINST POVERTY

'CAP's work amongst the poor and marginalised in the UK is inspirational and really needed at this time. We believe in a God who changes lives and through this charity, many desperate people have encountered the love of God in a practical and life-transforming way. These testimonies represent just a few of the people who have been offered hope where before there was none. CAP truly is transforming communities one life at a time.'

ANDY HAWTHORNE, CEO & Founder of The Message Trust

'Debt tears families apart and drives individuals to desperation. It is one of the most pressing problems facing our society today. I am so thankful for the work of CAP and the thousands of people whose lives have been transformed through that work. I am inspired when I read about people who have been given a way through their financial trauma, regained their dignity and, most importantly, received hope.'

ROB PARSONS, Care for the Family

I WOULD LIKE TO ORDER MY COPY OF JOURNEYS OF HOPE AT THE SPECIAL OFFER PRICE OF £3.99

- -

PLEASE COMPLETE IN BLOCK CAPITALS

My details:

Full Name: ....

Address: ....

....Postcode: ....

Telephone: ....

Email: ....

DESCRIPTION:	QUANTITY:	ITEM PRICE:	TOTAL:
JOURNEYS OF HOPE		£3.99	£
Please include P&P of: **£2** (orders of £0 – £9.99) **£3** (£10 – £19.99) **£5** (£20 – £29.99) **£6.50** (£30 – £39.99) **£8** (£40 upwards)	TOTAL COST FOR BOOKS:		£
	POSTAGE COST:		£
	DONATION TO CAP:		£
	TOTAL:		£

☐ **I enclose a cheque** (please make cheques payable to Christians Against Poverty)

☐ **Please debit my card:**

Card number: __ __ __ __ __ __ __ __ __ __ __ __ __ __ __ __

Expiry date: __ __ / __ __   Start Date: __ __ / __ __

Security Code: __ __ __ (last 3 digits on signature strip) Switch Issue Nº: __ __

Please post this form to CAP, Jubilee Mill, North Street, Bradford, BD1 4EW